KISSING
KILIMANJARO

KISSING
KILIMANJARO

LEAVING IT ALL

ON TOP
OF AFRICA

DANIEL DORR

THE MOUNTAINEERS BOOKS

THE MOUNTAINEERS BOOKS
is the nonprofit publishing arm of The Mountaineers Club, an
organization founded in 1906 and dedicated to the exploration,
preservation, and enjoyment of outdoor and wilderness areas.

1001 SW Klickitat Way, Suite 201, Seattle, WA 98134

© 2010 by Daniel Dorr

All rights reserved

First edition, 2010
No part of this book may be reproduced in any form, or by any
electronic, mechanical, or other means, without permission in writing
from the publisher.

Distributed in the United Kingdom by Cordee, www.cordee.co.uk

Manufactured in the United States of America

Copy editor: Amy Smith Bell
Book design and cartography: John Barnett/4 Eyes Design
All photographs by author unless credited otherwise.
Author photo: Lisa Dorr

Library of Congress Cataloging-in-Publication Data
Dorr, Daniel.
  Kissing Kilimanjaro : leaving it all on top of Africa / by Daniel Dorr.
— 1st ed.
    p. cm.
  ISBN 978-1-59485-370-8 (trade pbk.) — ISBN 978-1-59485-371-5
(ebook)
  1. Hiking—Tanzania—Kilimanjaro, Mount. 2. Mountaineering—
Tanzania—Kilimanjaro, Mount. 3. Dorr, Daniel—Travel—Tanzania—
Kilimanjaro (Mount) 4. Kilimanjaro, Mount (Tanzania)—Guidebooks.
5. Kilimanjaro, Mount (Tanzania)—Description and travel. I. Title.
  GV199.44.T342D67 2010
  796.510678'26—dc22
                            2010015580

ISBN (paperback): 978-1-59485-370-8
ISBN (e-book): 978-1-59485-371-5

FOR LISA

CONTENTS

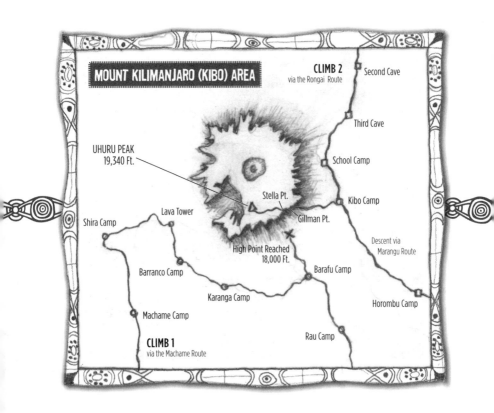

MOUNT KILIMANJARO (KIBO) AREA

CLIMB 2
via the Rongai Route

Second Cave

Third Cave

School Camp

UHURU PEAK
19,340 Ft.

Stella Pt.

Kibo Camp

Gillman Pt.

Lava Tower

Descent via
Marangu Route

Shira Camp

High Point Reached
18,000 Ft.

Barranco Camp

Barafu Camp

Karanga Camp

Horombu Camp

Machame Camp

Rau Camp

CLIMB 1
via the Machame Route

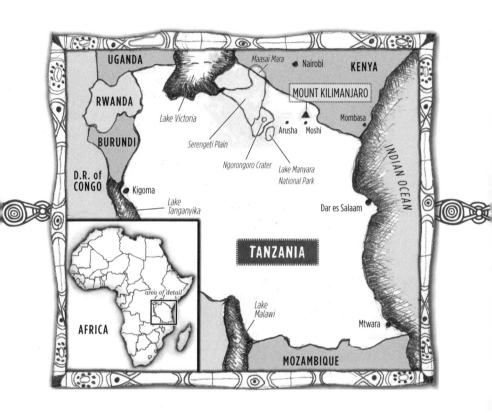

UGANDA

KENYA

RWANDA

BURUNDI

D.R. of
CONGO

Maasai Mara

Nairobi

MOUNT KILIMANJARO

Lake Victoria

Mombasa

Arusha   Moshi

Serengeti Plain

Ngorongoro Crater

Lake Manyara
National Park

Kigoma

Lake
Tanganyika

Dar es Salaam

INDIAN OCEAN

TANZANIA

AFRICA

area of detail

Lake
Malawi

Mtwara

MOZAMBIQUE

Mount Kilimanjaro, the highest point on the African continent
(Photograph by David Macready)

1

Anything for a Beautiful Brunette

I used to wonder what would ever possess anyone to trudge up a mountainside on the far sides of the planet, into harsh, frigid winds and thin air, thousands of feet above sea level. For decades men have died trying to reach Earth's highest points, to survive in places where humans were clearly not meant to endure. Was it for the glory of standing where few had dared to tread? Was it to test oneself against the elements and one's own inner weakness? Or was it simply another way to impress women?

For me it was a little bit of everything. But if I'm really honest with myself, I probably did it to impress a beautiful woman. My journey to the top of Africa started in a small coffee shop in Laguna Beach, California. I was on a date with that woman—our first date actually. Lisa sat across the table from me, cupping her hands around a mug of hot cocoa. I couldn't stop gazing at her—her long dark hair, deep brown eyes, and a smile that made me slightly dizzy. I had known her for almost ten years. Lisa and I had met in Japan right after college, where we were both teaching English as part of an exchange program in the early 1990s.

At the time I was in the middle of a long-term relationship, so I became Lisa's "safe" guy friend—someone she knew wouldn't hit on her at every opportunity. Together we explored the country, and over the course of a year we became close.

After that year of adventures, however, our paths separated. I returned to the United States to start my "real life" while Lisa stayed in Japan for another year. She moved to Switzerland to study French for a few months before finally returning to her home state of Hawaii, where she worked in a scuba shop. I moved around as well. My relationship had ended, and I decided on New York City as the place to start my career in the high-tech industry. I soon joined the other techies in San Jose, California, however, flocking to Silicon Valley for the Internet revolution. Lisa and I had stayed in touch throughout all these years, with infrequent letters and even less frequent phone calls. We couldn't help but feel inspired by each other's adventures and life changes, so we'd kept the connection alive.

Everything changed in 2001, when Lisa settled in Laguna Beach, California—only four hundred miles away! We started to talk on the phone more frequently, rebuilding our friendship. The calls eventually got longer and the bond grew stronger. One Friday evening as we were chatting late into the night, catching up on old flames and failed relationships, Lisa posed a question: "Dan, how come you and I have never dated?"

I was stumped, speechless. We had been friends living on opposite sides of the world for so long that the thought had never really crossed my mind. But a week later I was on a plane to Laguna Beach to find out if there was that kind of chemistry. We spent the day playing "remember when," reminiscing about our free-spirited travels across Japan. That evening, sipping our hot cocoa, we dreamed together about all the places we wanted to see: Alaska, Machu Picchu, New Zealand. The list went on.

Then Lisa uttered five fateful words: "I want to climb Kilimanjaro."

"That's perfect!" I blurted out, without thinking anything through. "I've been thinking about doing that for a long time." Her warm smile melted my decision-making skills. "Let's do it," I said in all seriousness. "Let's climb Kilimanjaro together." And with that, I was committed. Granted, if Lisa had suggested that we drive sled dogs across Antarctica, I probably would have signed on to that just as eagerly.

Climbing Kilimanjaro. It wasn't such a crazy idea, really. In 1980, American businessman and amateur mountaineer Richard Bass decided to climb to the highest point on each of the seven continents. He completed his task when he reached the summit of Mount Everest only five years later, sparking a new competition among the great mountaineers. Suddenly they all had to demonstrate their prowess by copying Bass. By 2003 a hundred climbers had joined his elite "Seven Summits" club.

While towering 19,340 feet above sea level, Kilimanjaro is by far the most attainable of the Seven Summits and is frequently the first one people attempt. Climbing it requires no special mountaineering skills, training, or equipment, and can be achieved at a reasonable expense. This "everyman's Everest" is a mecca for aspiring mountaineers, adventure tourists, and guys like me who just don't know when to shut up.

I had always dreamed of seeing Africa. It was one of those majestic, mysterious places I wanted to visit before I died. I'd talk about the continent in general terms at parties, with friends, or on airplanes. But the reality of making such a journey seemed too far out of reach, too remote, too exotic, or just too expensive. It was a "someday" kind of place.

I wasn't lying to Lisa about wanting to climb Kilimanjaro, though. In fact, the seed for this idea had been planted three years earlier by a fiery French coworker of mine, Delphine. She had traveled the globe—from Africa to Peru to Southeast Asia and other exotic locations on my "someday" list. I was intrigued by how she had managed to visit all these places with a limited budget and a limited number of vacation days. And where did she get the nerve to just get up and go? Delphine had climbed Kilimanjaro a few years before I met her. Sure it had been a challenging climb, she explained, but certainly possible. And then Delphine said something magical: "Kilimanjaro was a life-changing experience."

Hearing her talk about the climb made it seem feasible, even for a weekend warrior like me. Nonetheless, the idea of scaling a dormant volcano remained daunting. I wasn't a professional adventurer, I was a recreationalist. On weekends my friends and I would often escape the BMWs and concrete shopping malls of Silicon Valley to explore the sandstone rock formations of the Santa Cruz mountains. While we belayed each other off fifty-foot boulders, we'd dream about tackling a big wall in Yosemite. By sunset, however, we were eating burritos at Abuelos and relaxing with a cold beer. Sometimes we'd spend a long weekend rambling through the rolling granite of the Sierra Nevada. As we huffed and puffed up rocky slopes, we chatted about big mountains we might climb someday, like Kilimanjaro. But by Monday morning, my showered and shaved self would pull into the office parking lot in my gray Honda Accord. I'd sit at my desk, drinking company-supplied coffee and catching up with my coworkers. I wasn't a real mountain climber. I just played one on weekends.

But why *couldn't* I climb Kilimanjaro? The question nagged at me. I was a reasonably fit thirty-two-year-old. I could walk uphill. I'd slept in a tent. I knew how to gesture for food in a foreign country.

It was Lisa who gave me the final push I needed. Her bravery and sense of adventure inspired me. I may have been a dabbler in the mountains, but she was a complete novice. She had spent the vast majority of her life in the toasty and tranquil comfort of Hawaii. She had never been camping, had never climbed a mountain, and had never slept in a tent. She didn't even own a winter jacket or hiking boots. Worse still, she'd never heard of Gore-Tex.

Perhaps this fact should have concerned me. It didn't. I'd traveled with Lisa before. I knew she was adventurous and could handle almost any challenge. And she really is very pretty. If she thought she could climb Kilimanjaro, who was I to disagree?

I began asking around, looking for anyone, anywhere, who had done something similar to what Lisa and I planned. It didn't take long to find plenty of people who had climbed the mountain. I went hiking with the Sierra Club and met three veterans of Africa's highest peak. A coworker overheard me talking about Kilimanjaro and told me he'd made the climb. With his potbelly and diminutive, somewhat elfish figure, he bore more resemblance to a leprechaun than an alpinist. I was half his age, and at six-feet-four inches I towered over him. Surely, if Larry had climbed Kilimanjaro, I could too.

I was beginning to think I was the only person who hadn't been to the top of Kilimanjaro.

Still living four hundred miles apart, Lisa and I began preparing for our upcoming conquest. I was now visiting her in Laguna Beach almost every weekend. During the work week I would come home to my tiny studio apartment in San Jose and obsess over the details of the climb, trying to gather as much information as I could. On Friday afternoons I'd fly south to Laguna and we'd review our individual findings while strolling the beach or enjoying a brunch of German apple pancakes. We bought a copy of Cameron M. Burns's *Kilimanjaro and Mount Kenya: A Climbing and Trekking Guide* and read it cover-to-cover, highlighting key bits of information and filling the margins with questions and ideas for further discussion. We surfed the Web, spoke to outfitters, and attended local talks. We pored over maps, discussed routes, and wrote out a training program. With each step and each scrap of new information, the mountain was moving just a little bit closer, becoming a little bit more reachable.

There are five preferred routes to the summit of Kilimanjaro. The two most popular are the Marangu and Machame routes. Marangu is the shortest, requiring only five days to reach the summit, but that means little time for adjusting to altitude. We heard that only one in ten climbers on the Marangu Route actually makes it to the top. Most ascend too fast and are forced to turn back by searing headaches and vomiting brought on by altitude sickness. That didn't sound too appealing. This route is frequently called the "Tourist Route" or "Coca-Cola Route" because climbers sleep in huts instead of tents and chocolate, soda, and beer is available for sale at each camp. Sharing a hut with slumbering, smelly, snoring tourists who'd had a few too many beers at ten thousand feet wasn't what we were looking for. Lisa and I were prepared to share our body odors only with each other. Besides, we didn't want to be tourists: we wanted to take the road less traveled.

We decided on the Machame Route, sometimes referred to as the "Whisky Route" for its "intoxicating views." At least that's what the brochures said. It would be a seven-day climb, taking us through all the eco-zones—from rain forest to heather, moorland to alpine meadow, and finally to alpine desert. The trail traversed around the side of Kilimanjaro, which would give us two days to acclimate to the altitude and see more of the mountain. The other three routes—Lemosho, Rongai, and Shira—sounded interesting, but we found few outfitters who offered those climbs. We wanted to get off the beaten track, but not too far off.

Kilimanjaro is such a huge land mass that it actually creates its own weather patterns, making it possible to climb it any time of the year without suffering too much from seasonal rains. However, that isn't the case *off* the mountain; we read stories of clients getting stuck in mud during the heavy seasonal downpours. The rainy seasons extend from October through December and March through July. We decided on a September climb, at the tail end of the summer dry season, to avoid the rain and (we hoped) the crowds.

Now that we knew when and where, our next major question was how. We needed to find an outfitter who didn't balk at our meager budget. Because most certified and well-known American outfitters were out of our price range, I decided to check into the uncertified, unknown outfitters. We identified a reputable company based in Tanzania. In a lengthy email, I explained what we wanted, our climbing skill level, our budget, and our desired plans. I asked for more details and requested a few references. The response was two lines, with some sample itineraries and a packing list attached. Although the list was moderately helpful, the response didn't answer half of my questions.

I tried again, this time highlighting my questions in a bulleted list. The outfitter's response was another series of short one- or two-word answers, along with the same attachments. After several more exchanges, it became clear that we had a failure to communicate. Email could not penetrate the cultural and language barriers between us. But I bit my tongue and kept at it. Our messages went back and forth for two months before I finally got all the answers to my questions and we agreed on a reasonable price for the climb. Being on a tight budget, my patience was expendable—our money was not.

Originally Lisa and I had planned just to climb Kilimanjaro, nothing more. But this was a once-in-a-lifetime trip; it seemed shortsighted to travel all that distance and miss Africa's celebrated wildlife. Despite limited funds and vacation days, we decided to dig ourselves in a little deeper. We signed up for a four-day safari to Lake Manyara, the Serengeti, and the Ngorongoro Crater.

Next, we got our arms shot full of dead pathogens—cholera, hepatitis, malaria, tetanus, typhoid, and yellow fever—to protect our American immune systems from the upcoming onslaught of unfamiliar antagonists. We sent our deposits to the outfitters in Africa, we bought airline tickets, we renewed our passports, and we acquired the necessary visas. Four months after that fateful evening at Diedrich's Coffee Shop, we were booked. There was no turning back: Lisa and I were going to climb a 750,000-year-old mound of dirt and volcanic rock!

Kilimanjaro wasn't always so far away. One hundred eighty million years ago, the continents as we know them didn't exist. They were jammed together in one big land mass we've since named Gondwanaland. Slowly the continental plates separated and the various land masses ground across the earth's crust, expelling tremendous heat and pressure as they shimmied along. Africa, however, held its ground and has been percolating in one spot for more than two hundred million years, unable to vent the molten furnace beneath. The relentless buildup of heat has pushed the land mass an average of a thousand feet higher than the other continents.

The pressure became too much 750,000 years ago, and three massive volcanic vents ripped open in East Africa. They shot hot magma into the sky and slowly stacked layer upon layer of molten rock, eventually forming three mountains: Shira, Mawenzi, and Kibo. The Shira cone was the first to burst out of the fertile plain but soon collapsed on itself and became extinct. Mawenzi formed several miles away before Kibo rose up between them both and fused them into one massive mountain. Today the Kibo cone is the summit portion of the combined mass known as Mount Kilimanjaro. After Kibo usurped its neighbors, it spewed forth lava and ash until 360,000 years ago. For thousands of years lava rolled over the rim and filled in the gap between the separate volcanoes, creating the current saddle between the Kibo and Mawenzi formations. The whole mountain eventually leveled off at 19,340 feet above sea level. It last erupted 100,000 years ago and has sat quietly ever since.

Kilimanjaro is different from many of the world's giant summits. It's not a spire in a rolling chain of mountains.

It stands alone, a sentinel on the East African plain—the largest freestanding mountain in the world, covering more than nine hundred square miles. It is a long, massive mound of rock that almost anyone with enough time and energy can ascend. The three original volcanoes aren't distinguishable any more as separate entities. The Kibo cone forms the flattop summit made famous in pictures, books, and movies. Shira, an extended lava plateau along the southwestern side, can be easily reached in two days of hiking. Mawenzi, a craggy rock formation jutting out from the mountain's eastern side, is today a crumbling monument when compared with the more glorious days of old when it stood alone.

A local Chagga legend explains how these great peaks softened from treacherous lava formations to the more hospitable mountain. Long ago, there were two neighboring giant volcanoes in East Africa: Kibo was the taller and grander, while Mawenzi was smaller and constantly jealous of his more impressive neighbor (Shira was no longer a separate peak by this time). Kibo was also the more industrious of the two, and Mawenzi was forever taking advantage of him. Mawenzi would frequently let the fire go out of his hearth and come begging Kibo for help and food. The generous Kibo would always stop his work of pounding dried bananas with a pestle and mortar to gather coals for Mawenzi and send him off with some sustenance. Mawenzi was a terrible cook and always loved what Kibo would prepare. Sometimes he would let his hearth go out two or three times in a row to test Kibo's patience.

One day, after letting his coals burn out, Mawenzi sought out Kibo. But Kibo was not at home, so Mawenzi decided to help himself to what was there. Dragging the hot embers back to his hearth, Mawenzi grumbled and complained about having to do his own cooking. As Kibo returned, he saw from a distance the red glow of his coals being taken. He found his hearth barren and all his hot coals missing. He was so angry he grabbed his pestle, ran to Mawenzi, and struck a crashing blow on the head, rendering Mawenzi with the jagged formation we see today and himself dormant.

Over the years Kilimanjaro has become synonymous with exotic adventure. Yet, surprisingly, the powerful name has no agreed-on translation. In the local Chagga dialect it can mean "Mountain of Greatness" or even "Mountain of Caravans." In Swahili, Kilimanjaro might be "Shining Mountain," "Mountain of the Cold Devils," or even the unlikely "Little Mountain." The nearby Maasai tribes call it the "White Mountain." In the end, the translation many people have settled on is from the Swahili word *kilima*, which means "top of the hill," and *njaro*, which presumably refers in some way to the snow. But no one really knows for sure.

The origin of the name didn't matter to Lisa and me: either way, we were up for an adventure.

Backpacking in Yosemite

2

The Romantic Glow of a Halogen Headlamp

As lisa and I started training for our climb up Mount Kilimanjaro, we realized that she had none of the necessary clothing or equipment to attempt a trek of this nature. She spent her weekdays wearing business casual and her weekends in shorts, t-shirts, and flip-flops. She had no thermal socks, long underwear, waterproof shell jacket, gloves, mittens, or even a knit hat. She didn't own a backpack, trekking poles, hydration system, water purification tablets, or flashlight of any kind. Before we could start training, we had to go shopping.

For a budding gearhead like me, the climb represented a magnificent opportunity: more stuff! I had been a camper for years, and most of my equipment was adequate for weekend adventures in California's Sierra Nevada. But Africa? Surely, I needed new gear for a quest of that magnitude. Outfitting Lisa and adding to my own supply was like Christmas, except we had to pay for the presents.

I scoped out all the camping and climbing stores in the greater San Francisco Bay Area. I rummaged through outlet stores, sniffed my way along shelves at sporting good depots, and loitered in REI, Any Mountain, the North Face outlet, and every local outfitter I could find. I slept with the REI and Sierra Trading Post catalogs next to me and surfed the Internet for bargains. After weeks of research, Lisa and I decided we were ready to go shopping. Our first task was to find Lisa a pair of hiking boots. After scanning the women's shoe wall at the Anaheim REI, we narrowed our search down to three different pairs. Lisa stomped around the store for a while in each pair and then looked up at me.

"What do you think?" she asked.

"What do *I* think?"

"Yeah, what do you think? Do these fit?"

"Um . . . you're the one wearing the boots," I said, a bit confused. "What do *you* think?"

"Oh, *I* don't know," she said casually. "I've never worn hiking boots before."

Growing up in Hawaii, Lisa rarely had occasion to wear shoes of any kind, let alone hiking boots. To her, everything she tried on felt constricting and heavy. I had grown up in New York, however, spending my winters climbing over snowbanks and shoveling snow. Boots felt natural to me, warm and secure. Lisa eventually narrowed it down to two pairs: one felt too tight and another felt looser. I was worried that the looser boots might give her blisters, but in the end she chose them. (By the way, she never got any blisters.)

Lisa and I had officially been dating for six months. The weekdays in between my weekend visits were feeling longer and more unbearable. One Saturday night we sat on a local beach and listened to the ocean tickle the shore. Lisa told me how tired she was of her customer-service job and that it was time for a change, even though she didn't know what to do next.

Now it was *my* turn for a bold suggestion: "Why don't you move in with me in San Jose?"

Lisa accepted the proposal and a month later we loaded up her Geo Metro with her growing supply of adventure gear and drove the eight hours up the coast. Her flip-flops took up residence outside my front door, her clothes nestled into the nooks and crannies in my tiny studio apartment, and her climbing stash piled high in the corner, comingling with my own. In the evenings we would wander down the street to REI or Any Mountain, dreaming about our upcoming adventure and perusing the travel book section. We searched for items we might have overlooked. We tried hydration packs of various sizes and capacities. We clunked around with various trekking poles and played with headlamps. Lisa crawled into sleeping bags, testing them for warmth and comfort. Every time she started talking about down versus synthetic materials or LED versus halogen headlamps, I fell just a little bit more in love with her.

Throughout our gear runs, I couldn't resist acquiring a few things as well. Some items were pretty run-of-the-mill—stuff like trekking poles and wool socks. Others were a bit more fun, such as an LED headlamp that had both white and red lights (the red lights help maintain night vision). We found waterless bath soap and shampoo to keep clean on the trail (after all, we were still dating), and even antimicrobial boxer shorts that claimed to virtually eliminate odors. Those I had to try. I put them to the test and wore the boxers for a full week, never changing them or taking them off (except to shower). I wore them to bed, to work, to the gym—just about everywhere. (I'm pretty sure that at this point Lisa began to question the wisdom of moving in with me.) At the end of the week, I had to admit it: they were the most comfortable and least aromatic pair of underwear I had ever worn.

Lisa pauses to pose while rock climbing in California

Now that Lisa and I were fully outfitted, we were ready for a trial run. On a Saturday morning in June, with the heat rippling off the pavement and the sun frying the dry grass along the highway, we drove north, headed for Mount Shasta. We had booked a three-day summit climb with Sierra Wilderness Seminars. From a distance Shasta appeared to be little more than a large hill. With each mile, however, it grew larger and more impressive, its peak breaking through the ring of clouds that had obscured it. The mountain stood 14,179 feet above sea level, a giant mound of volcanic rock towering over the landscape. Lava flows from generations ago stretched out in every direction, giant ridges like fingers extending from the summit. By now the snow had melted from the peak but hadn't left the mountain completely. Large white swaths hid in the deep valleys between rock creases, protected from the sun and wind. We were supposed to climb up that snow-and-rock colossus? As each moment passed I gained a healthy respect for the altitude and the mountain.

We met the other climbers and our guide, Stephan, at the parking lot at 6,950 feet. As we panted in the already thin air, Stephan handed each of us a small paper bag.

"You'll need one of these," he explained. "You have to pack your waste out."

At first I thought it was some kind of joke guides play on naive clients. But, alas, it was true. With no soil, grass, trees, or vegetation at the higher elevations, Shasta's rocky slopes can't absorb the human waste left by the estimated 15,000 climbers who attempt the summit every year. Thus the park service has devised an ingenious system to help people carry out their waste. Stephan explained that all climbers are provided with a large sheet of paper with a target on it, a paper bag with some cat litter, and a larger plastic bag. The concept is simple: hit the target, dump some cat litter on it, fold it up, stuff it in the paper bag, and then stuff the paper bag into the plastic bag. After all this the park service hopes climbers will have no problem stuffing the plastic, waste-filled bag into a backpack and carrying it around for a few days.

On Day 1, Stephan guided us up Shasta's steep lower slopes, preparing us for the summit ascent. "The best way to combat altitude sickness is to drink lots of water," he said. "Clear and copious is the way to go. You should expect to drink at least four liters a day. In fact, I never leave my sleeping bag in the morning without drinking at least one full liter of water."

He helped us keep this little weekend adventure in perspective. "The most important thing to remember is that 'the summit' isn't reaching the top of the mountain. 'The summit' is getting back to the car safely at the end of the climb. My biggest priority is that you get back safe. Reaching the top is just a bonus."

On our second day we tramped in the deep snow and learned key mountaineering skills. With our guide's careful instruction, we learned how to climb with crampons, self-arrest with ice axes, and glissade down steep snowfields. *This is the stuff they do on Rainier, Denali, and Everest,* I told myself. Lisa and I were becoming real mountain climbers.

"This is my kind of alpinism," Lisa beamed. As she practiced glissading, she sat in the snow and tobogganed down the hill on her butt, gripping her ice ax along the right side of her body for stability and control. To stop, she lifted the head of the ax up and drove the point of the shaft down into the snow until the friction slowed her to a halt. That part didn't thrill her, but she loved the sledding at high speeds. "Who knew mountain climbing could be so much fun?" she asked.

Stephan was a fountain of knowledge and he openly shared his mountaineering expertise with us, even the more personal bits. As we got ready to turn in that night, he explained one critical aspect of alpinism: how climbers relieve themselves in the frigid nights at high altitudes. "I always bring a pee bottle," he said with a smile. "I haven't gotten out of my sleeping bag to go to the latrine in over fifteen years." He held up a somewhat tattered and currently empty bottle.

Thankfully, I didn't need to test Stephan's suggestion that night. It was the morning of Day 3, and we were up and climbing at 3:00 AM. Stephan wanted to make sure we were off the summit by 12:00 PM, before the afternoon sun had melted too much snow, which would cause poor traction and rockfall conditions.

Stephan split up the group based on his assessment of our pace and endurance. He took the faster climbers with him, while the assistant guide, Brian, took Lisa and me. The first few hours were painfully tedious. The snowpack was steep, forcing us to zigzag back and forth endlessly in the dark. The hours passed and we continued to plod along. By the time the sun had started to provide a bit of light, Stephan and his group were well ahead of Lisa, Brian, and me. Obviously, our trio was making slow progress.

Lisa's legs were more accustomed to swimming in the ocean and running in sand than climbing snow-covered mountains. She marched along slowly as she puffed in the crisp mountain air. As the morning progressed, I noticed that her body had only one speed. No matter how steep the pitch of the mountain or how much Brian or I tried to push her, Lisa continued at her own slow-and-steady pace. This didn't mean that she was tired or needed to turn back. She was just chipping away at the mountain at her own rate.

As we slogged up the mountain, a pattern developed: Brian would go a few hundred feet ahead and then plop down in the snow, waiting impatiently until I arrived. Once I reached him, we would both wait for Lisa. "Hi! How's it going?" she'd ask cheerfully when she caught up. I'd smile back or try to offer some encouragement while Brian huffed off, beginning the whole cycle again. I was becoming frustrated with Lisa and her slow pace. I knew I could go faster. My legs still felt strong. Brian was even more annoyed with our slow progress. He didn't seem interested in adjusting his style to match Lisa's or mine.

After seven hours of climbing, we ascended through a small valley between the lava folds and came out onto an open platform of rock and snow, with a tall mound on the other side. We were now more than 13,000 feet above sea level, with almost 30 percent less oxygen than we were accustomed to down below. My head ached and I was slightly nauseous from the altitude. I remembered what Stephan had said about hydration and gulped down more water. But we weren't at the summit yet. We were at the base of Misery Hill, a false summit. The true top was another half mile away, more than 500 feet higher. It was almost noon, the time Stephan had demanded that everyone head down, no matter where we were.

Brian looked up Misery Hill and back at Lisa. "You've got to go faster if you want to make it to the summit."

"This is my pace," Lisa explained, standing firm in the face of Brian's increasing snarkiness. Ever since I've known her, Lisa has had a strong sense of self and been fiercely independent. If Brian didn't like her pace that was too bad for him.

"It's not fast enough," he retorted. "You'll have to stay

here." And then he looked at me. "You can make a break for it if you want to."

When Lisa and I had originally talked about climbing Shasta and then Kilimanjaro, we had agreed to stay together no matter what. After all, we were in love. But now I was just a half mile from the top and I had contracted a bad case of summit fever. The idea of turning around when I was so close and had energy left gnawed at me. I knew I could do it. I wanted to do it, even if that meant going with an annoying guide.

"You go ahead," Lisa said, smiling at me. "I'll be fine here." She was sitting with her back to a pile of rocks that acted as a barrier against the wind. It was a well-protected and even comfortable spot. Nonetheless, I didn't like the idea of leaving her by herself. I looked around for any excuse and saw several other climbers passing or resting nearby. *She won't really be alone,* I told myself.

"It's okay," she insisted. "Stephan will be coming back in a few minutes with the other group anyway." I hesitated for a second, then gave in. I kissed Lisa good-bye, grabbed my pack, and Brian and I were off.

We passed Stephan at the top of Misery Hill and kept going. On the far side of the hill, I picked up my pace to almost a jog and rushed across the last hundred feet to the final rock formation. My chest heaved as I gulped in the thin air. I scrambled up the last thirty feet of cold granite to reach the official top, the crown of the mountain.

I had climbed Mount Shasta.

I paused and took it all in. It was everything I had hoped it would be. All of Northern California and Southern Oregon swept out before me as the sun shone down on the rolling landscape below. Rocks, snow, and ice descended in all directions and the Cascade Range in the distant north seemed small from my monumental perch. I hugged the rock and sucked in the summit air. I had done it. I had overcome the snow, the cold, the steepness, the rocks, and even the lack of oxygen to reach one of the highest points in the state of California. I was sitting at 14,179 feet above sea level. I had hiked for more than nine hours straight and had pushed myself like never before.

Slowly my euphoria began to subside, though. I realized I was still nauseous and that my headache had gotten worse with my last impatient push. Brian took my camera and snapped the ceremonial picture of me at the summit, beaming with satisfaction. Then we rushed back down to find Lisa waiting patiently for us on the plateau just as Stephan was starting to leave with his group.

I felt a deep sense of pride and, I admit, a pretty inflated ego. I had summited my first real mountain and (I hoped) impressed my girlfriend in the process. But I also began to realize that much of my success was due to Lisa's slower pace. Left to my own devices, I suspect my competitive nature would have driven me too hard, and I would have been exhausted by the time we reached Misery Hill. Lisa's smooth and constant pace was unhurried, allowing my body time to adjust without crashing. This was exactly the kind of pacing I would need on Kilimanjaro.

"I'm glad you got your summit experience," she said. "I was pretty happy camped out here." Her smile beamed under her oversized helmet and knit hat. She was having the time of her life just being on the mountain. Unlike me, Lisa didn't need to summit to complete the trip—just being there was enough for her. I couldn't help but fall a little more in love with her.

After a short break it was time to go. We sat down in the snow and glissaded more than 2,000 feet down the steep mountain at harrowing speeds. By the time we reached our campsite, Lisa was absolutely beaming. "I don't need the summit when I get to glissade," she said with a grin.

We packed up our things and began the long march off the mountain. We were off the snow now and meandered for the next few miles along the barren gravel path until we entered the forest once again. The others had gone on ahead, and Lisa and I were alone in the silent woods, just the two of us. It was late afternoon and the low sun gave way to a cool breeze that slithered through the snow-filled mountain valleys. The scent of pine filled the air, and trees, meadows, and wildflowers welcomed us safely back. Our first alpine adventure was behind us—and it had been a success.

Local fruit stand in Moshi, Tanzania

3

Tourist Class

Three months after our Mount Shasta test climb, Lisa and I boarded our flight to Africa. I was ready. I was an alpinist after all, a weekend warrior no longer! I had successfully ascended Shasta, straddling a summit more than 14,000 feet above sea level—higher than I'd ever been without the aid of a pilot, a flight attendant, and several hundred Boeing employees. The air had been thin up there, the slope steep, and the wind cold. But I had done it. Although Lisa's pace had initially frustrated me, it was her slow-and-steady style that had enabled me to conserve my energy for the final summit push. Thanks to her, I had made it with enthusiasm to spare, suffering only mild nausea and a minor headache from the altitude.

Now that we were on our way to Africa, doubt crept in. Looking back at our somewhat spotty training program, were we ready? The training had started out strong, with jogs through the neighborhood every other evening and a visit to the gym for cardio and free weights three times a week. But after Shasta my confidence had grown and my determination had waned. Lisa and I had spent more time *dreaming* about our upcoming African adventure than we had actually *training* for it. We had also started to talk more and more about what our life might look like *after* Kilimanjaro.

I knew I wanted our journeys together to continue. And so, a month before our departure, we stood among the majestic redwood trees of Muir Woods and I asked Lisa to marry me. Thankfully, she accepted and I spent the following weeks elated, basking in the glow of my future wife instead of dripping sweat all over a StairMaster. Now in flight, as we crossed the Atlantic, a small pang of hesitation settled in: were we truly prepared for Kilimanjaro? I reminded myself of our successes on Mount Shasta and quickly brushed away any lingering concerns.

It took two full days of flying, with only thirty-one inches of legroom between us and our fellow travelers, before we finally touched down in Kenya. We arrived at Nairobi Jomo Kenyatta International Airport, landing on the steaming tarmac just after sunset. The day's heat oozed off the ground and the scent of local fires and diesel fumes saturated us. The sky cast an orange glow across the rolling plains, and we could feel the vast expanse around us. We were finally here. After so long, Kenya felt strangely welcoming, as if we were coming to visit a long lost relative we had heard so much about but never actually met.

We made our way into the sparse cement airport, past a few small curio shops and through customs and passport control. We hoisted our massive bags and backpacks onto a luggage trolley and shoved it out of the protected baggage claim area and smack into life in Kenya. Immediately we were swarmed by solicitors assaulting us with offers for every service imaginable. They pressed in on us from all sides.

"You need taxi? I take you."

"Safari parks. See best parks right here."

"Where your hotel?"

After two days nestled inside the dark, quiet cocoon of a 747, this onslaught was too much for our jet-lagged bodies. We shoved our way through the crowd and found an out-of-the-way sanctuary to catch our breath. Leaving Lisa to guard our luggage, I stepped outside the airport, hoping to find a calmer scene. The crowd out there was even worse. More people swarmed, offering rides, safaris, hotels, and countless other services I couldn't make out over the shouting and pleading. I fought myself free and retreated back into the airport. Eventually I found a taxi service office inside, which, because of the actual counter, somehow seemed more reputable. We paid a fifteen-dollar fee for the ride to our hotel, were handed a small yellow slip of paper, and told to step outside.

I steeled myself for the onslaught as we staggered back out the door, holding up our tiny yellow paper as if it were some kind of magic amulet. Within seconds a driver emerged from the crowd and snatched the paper. "Come. I take you," he commanded. Not knowing what else to do, we followed him. The driver dumped our bags into the trunk and we were off.

He shot into the graying night as we sat in the back of the car, clutching the door handles, wondering if we'd made a horrible mistake.

"We're going to the Stanley Hotel," I pointed out.

"Yes, I know," he replied, holding the small piece of paper with that exact information on it.

"Um, yes. We've already paid our fare, right?"

"Yes, I know," he replied again as he careened onto the main road and accelerated toward the city.

The sun was casting its final glow across the landscape and night was rapidly descending. I could see the urban lights glowing in the distance as darkness covered us. We cruised along a service road on the outskirts of town, past small warehouses and office buildings. Behind them the savanna extended into the shadows. Every so often, we saw a group of men congregated by the side of an office building or around a small fire. There didn't appear to be any housing nearby, and I wondered what they were doing way out here. Perhaps they were waiting for work—not a surprise, given the city's past. Nairobi has been attracting locals for work opportunities since it was originally founded in 1899 as a supply point for the Uganda Railway that was being built from Mombasa to Uganda. Over time the settlement continued to grow and eventually became a British protectorate in 1907. In 1963, Kenya finally gained independence and named Nairobi as its young capital.

Today Nairobi is a place of beauty and contradictions. It's the only city in the world to house an actual game reserve—Nairobi National Park—within its borders and it is home to more species of birds than any other capital in the world. More than 3,000,000 human residents call the city their home today as well, many of them impoverished and living in shantytowns. Nairobi is only ninety miles south of the equator, but at 5,000 feet above sea level it has a surprisingly mild climate.

We were grateful for the cool evening air as we emerged safely from the taxi in front of the Stanley Hotel. The soft breeze wiped away some of our exhaustion. As we stepped into the spacious lobby, a friendly porter greeted us. "Welcome to the Stanley Hotel," he beamed.

It was exactly what we had imagined after watching Meryl Streep in *Out of Africa* too many times. This was colonial East Africa alive and kicking. The black-and-white checkered tile floor expanded across the lobby to the two long reception desks of dark wood, with handsome hosts standing behind them. In the lobby's center was a circular leather couch with a tall grandfather clock standing in the middle, a throwback to a time when most people didn't own a wristwatch. The understated simplicity of it all made the space even more attractive. There were no massive statues or overly ornate decorations. The room was sparsely adorned with little more than a few faded leather chairs, some landscape photos on the wall, and a few soft lights. But it bustled with activity and the feeling of important things happening. Within seconds we heard accents from Australia, Germany, Japan, North America, the United Kingdom, and other locales.

Staying at the Stanley Hotel was Lisa's present to herself. She'd heard of the hotel from others who had been to Nairobi and she just had to see it. The off-season rate was reasonable, and after only one minute in the lobby, we concluded this experience would be well worth the cost. We checked in and took the open-gate elevator to our room. The massive king-size bed dominated the far wall and beckoned us to sleep. But it wasn't time for that yet.

After dumping our belongings, hunger drove us back downstairs to the hotel restaurant. We dined in the open-air Thorn Tree Restaurant, just off the lobby, as the city's breeze scented the patio. I looked across the open terrace; it almost felt like the 1930s. Ernest Hemingway himself could have been sitting at the bar, amazing travelers with his stories of adventure. The Stanley has a bit of a reputation for inspiring many authors, including Elspeth Huxley, Colonel J. H. Patterson, and of course, Hemingway.

More recently, Bill Bryson visited Nairobi to write a short travel book for CARE International. However, he stayed down the street at the Holiday Inn.

After dinner I decided to try getting some local currency. We returned to the lobby and I asked the concierge where I could find a cash machine.

"There is a Standard Charter bank just down the street here, sir," he replied. "But it is dangerous for you to go out alone. Please let a porter go with you."

"We'll be fine," I answered, with my "I've lived in New York City" confidence.

"It is better," he urged. The concierge said something in Swahili and a petite young porter emerged to assist us. He was about five feet tall, with a gentle smile.

"Please come with me, sir."

Accompanied by our new bodyguard, we made our way down the dark street. It was 9:00 PM and the tired streetlights cast a weak glow on the sidewalk. It was quiet and the streets were mostly empty of traffic. Small groups of young men lounged and chatted with each other on porch steps and street corners. How would this diminutive porter, considerably smaller than either Lisa or I, provide us any kind of protection? If we had been walking down any other street in the world, it would have appeared that we were protecting *his* tiny form instead of the reverse. But he walked with the confidence of a man who could handle himself and had done so on previous occasions. The porter had almost a swagger in his movements. I later learned that many of the hotel porters are members of the Maasai tribe, famous for being fierce warriors and incredibly loyal. Many say it is impossible to bribe a Maasai and that they don't understand the concept of relenting once in battle. While this young man didn't wear the traditional red-and-black Maasai blanket over his shoulders, it was apparently clear to everyone on the street who he was. Our safety was all but assured.

Unfortunately, this is not the case for all visitors in Nairobi. In 2001 the United Nations International Civil Service Commission rated Nairobi as one of the most unsafe cities in the world. The head of one development agency cited the "notoriously high levels of violent armed robberies, burglaries, and car-jackings." The city's name comes from the Maasai word *enkarenairobi*, which means "cool waters." In recent years, however, it has been affectionately referred to as "Nai-robbery." As a protected guest, I didn't feel in danger. But the city did emit the atmosphere of a place trying to deal with tremendous urban growth, struggling to find its proper place in the world.

At last we were at the cash machine, but to my dismay, I discovered that it didn't work with my American bankcard. Lisa and I returned to our hotel room. Exhausted, we crashed for the night.

The next morning we checked out early to catch the Davanu Shuttle to Moshi, Tanzania. The sun was bright and seared into our jet-lagged eyes as we dragged our bags around the corner and down the sidewalk to the nearby bus stop. It was Sunday morning and the street was slowly filling up with cars. The sidewalks were gradually coming alive with pedestrians. As we lumbered down the sidewalk, a man walked up to me, pointed to Lisa, and asked, "Is she yours?" Lisa didn't hear him. We just kept walking.

We were greeted at the shuttle bus by Gibonga, the capable manager of this operation. We purchased our tickets with U.S. dollars and within seconds our bags were thrown into the air and caught by a young man on top of the bus. He tied everything down and announced they were ready to start. It was only a few minutes after the 8:30 AM scheduled departure time, and I told Gibonga how impressed I was with the punctuality.

"This is a tourist bus," he said. "We need to leave on time or the tourists don't like it."

"When does a local bus in Kenya leave?" I asked.

"When it's full."

While planning this trip, Lisa and I had thought that taking this cross-country bus to Tanzania would be a great way to go "local style." But as I stepped aboard, I could see how wrong we had been. All of the passengers were white, wearing khaki head to toe, as if we were headed out for a safari. In almost every seat sat couples holding their safari hats on their khaki-clad laps, faces smiling behind dark sunglasses and several layers of sunscreen. Over their heads cameras and backpacks rested neatly on the rack. The bus was clean, orderly, and air-conditioned. I immediately understood that this was not how the locals traveled. The bus snaked its way through the growing morning traffic and made a few more stops at other hotels before finally leaving the city proper. We rode down the one-lane highway and passed a shantytown with people digging in a nearby garbage pile, reminding me that we were, in fact, in a developing country.

One of the problems with travel today is that the traveler is practically teleported from one location to the next. Just two days ago I had woken up in California. This morning I rose in Nairobi, Kenya. Tomorrow I'd get up in Moshi, Tanzania. The reality of my current location hadn't caught up with me. I needed time to soak it all in and absorb my surroundings. Fortunately, the bus trip to

Tanzania would take six hours or more across the East African savanna.

The bus turned right onto another highway, with a road sign displaying ARUSHA 251KM. Underneath this was a large red-and-white Coke logo. Apparently, the company had funded a number of road signs in Kenya, in an effort to increase brand awareness. The reality of a region so poor that global consumer companies could fund some of the infrastructure was a bit much at 9:00 AM. But we were safe in our little tourist khaki cocoon and didn't need to think about the surrounding poverty. We sped down the road and watched Kenya pass us by.

Within an hour we had escaped the development of Nairobi and transitioned into equatorial East Africa. There were fewer buildings, and they were smaller and less modern. The people went from wearing shirts and slacks to Maasai men and boys wearing the traditional red-and-black blankets thrown over their bodies. Telephone poles were replaced by green acacia trees and the burnt savanna rolled on to the horizon. The sun was getting high in the vast blue sky. Golden grass spread out across the countryside, and small, thorny bushes popped up here and there.

This was the major road across Kenya to Tanzania. It was paved and smooth and hosted infrequent traffic. Every so often a freight truck would pass, or we'd speed by one of the local "buses" Gibonga had mentioned. They were small vans with enough seating for nine, but they were frequently packed with twenty or more riders. Young men hung out the side doors while women, children, and the elderly crammed inside. Each van had been spray-painted with a unique design of vivid colors and sayings. Some advertised hair salons or grocery stores. Others sought only to entertain or inspire onlookers. I could discern no pattern to the various artistic choices the drivers had made.

At the next town we were forced to wait as a herd of cows crossed in front of us. The village was made up of a few one-room, red-brick buildings protected by worn wooden-plank roofs. One appeared to be a general store and a group of men stood out front watching the world go by. I stared out the window at the local bus being loaded next to us. The back hatch was open and a young Maasai man was cramming a small kicking goat under the back seat. The goat, clearly unhappy with its quarters for the trip, screamed and flailed while the young man shoved. The rest of the passengers waited patiently as if this were a standard occurrence. I wondered what would happen if I tried to pack a goat under my seat on the tourist bus.

The farther we got from Nairobi, the more the Maasai became a part of our landscape. We passed Maasai boys wearing brown cloaks and carrying short herding sticks. They walked along the roadside directing their goats in the hot sun, or they rested under the shade of acacia trees. Young Maasai boys are often given the responsibility of tending the goats while the men have the harder task of tending the cattle herds. The Maasai are a proud people who have fought long and hard to keep their traditional way of life as the world has changed around them. It is believed that the Maasai people originally came down the Nile and eventually settled in East Africa. For thousands of years these pastoralists herded their cattle and goats around the region, following the rains and good grazing. But in the past century, Europeans arrived and created random country borders in the middle of the Maasai migration. More recently, vast tracts of grazing land were taken by the Kenyan and Tanzanian governments to create nature preserves to protect the dwindling wildlife populations. Over time more hotels have sprung up and more buses full of tourists have passed through the Maasai's traditional lands.

Maasai boys herding sheep in the Ngorongoro Conservation Area

And so the Maasai have learned to adapt. Some have gone to school and joined the new world while some have stayed in the villages and carried on the traditional herding lifestyle. Others have learned to walk the razor's edge between old and new ways. These are the ones who herd their goats on foot across the plains but don't have any problem stuffing them in the back of a passing truck if the opportunity arises.

By late morning our surroundings had completely transformed from the soot and colonialism of Nairobi to the natural, rugged beauty of the savanna. As the country unfolded outside the window, my new companions became the flattop acacia trees, large termite mounds, and unhurried tiny towns.

We were stopped at a military checkpoint in the next town, where the police were inspecting vehicles. I have no idea what they were searching for. They seemed to laze around and randomly select which cars to check. At the time I assumed it must have been part of a complicated sting operation. The more likely scenario is that the police were extorting bribes. But I was enjoying my savanna drive too much to allow such negative opinions to form of my host country, another advantage of going "tourist class." The town—three brick buildings built up along the roadside—was all that interrupted the plains around us. We queued behind the other cars and waited to be waved on.

I passed the time gazing out the window and taking in the local scenery. Eventually my eyes caught the rather fierce glare of a full-grown Maasai warrior. He stood by the side of the road, gripping a large spear and staring directly at me as if I had just insulted his sister. I am not too proud to say I felt more than a little intimidated by the fierce stare of a man who had, more than likely, killed a full-grown lion at the same age when I was wearing braces and feeling intimidated by girls. There was a darkness and intensity to his stare; he seemed to be looking *inside* me. His face was almost completely black except for his whitish-yellow eyes penetrating me.

I've been told that while traveling in foreign countries where I didn't speak the language, a smile was the best weapon in almost any situation. That thought sprang to mind as I squirmed under the warrior's gaze. It seemed ridiculous to smile at someone who was clearly not happy with my presence. But feeling protected in my little white bus and having no other ideas, I gave it a try. I turned back to the silent figure and returned his dark glare with a hesitant grin.

Almost immediately, the fierce warrior was transformed. His scowl vanished, and he grinned from ear to ear. His eyes beamed with delight and there was a welcoming in his smile. I think he'd have invited me over for milk (the staple drink for the Maasai) had we not been separated by the bus windows. I began to realize that my safety as a tourist-class traveler was costing me some real experiences.

The police waved our bus on, and my new friend vanished in the distance as we continued down the road. I spent the next hour looking out the window, greeting any small children, grown men, and elders I could see with the biggest smile I could muster. At each encounter I was awarded with a friendly grin and even a wave from time to time. I was finding long lost friends all the way across the continent and loving every minute of it.

At our official noon break, we were allowed some time to peruse a small tourist shop. I was looking at some wooden masks when the shopkeeper approached me. "That one means 'doctor,'" he informed me.

"Ahh," I replied, as if that was the exact information I was looking for.

"The next one means 'engagement,'" he offered. Each mask was beautifully carved and had a contorted face with decorative touches such as a headdress, earrings, or other markings. I could see no feature that might tie any specific mask to an occupation or event. But then, I hadn't grown up in Kenya and my frame of reference might not be the same.

"You from America?" he inquired.

This is a loaded question. During previous travels I've claimed to be Canadian, German, even Spanish once. These disguises were not out of fear of being attacked as much as wanting to avoid hours of political rhetoric or questions about New Coke, McDonalds, Starbucks, or any of the other blessings and curses my native country has bestowed on the world. But I was feeling quite at home in Kenya and didn't want to lie to my new friends.

"Yes, I'm from America."

"You be my distributor in the U.S.," he blurted. "I sell to you and you sell in the U.S. You make a lot of money. Give me your address and I contact you."

It was my first business proposal in Africa, not counting the gentleman who asked me if Lisa was "mine." I really wasn't sure what to make of it. As I stood there contemplating his offer, he continued his sales pitch.

"You make a lot of money. Very popular in U.S."

The more he pushed, the less interested I became. "I'll get back to you on that."

"Okay, I see you when you come back," he agreed, and was off to talk to other prospects.

While I was negotiating this possible career change with the manager, Lisa had been talking to some of the other employees. "Did you know the shop was set up to raise money to help Maasai girls go to school?" she asked. "I want to get something to support this." Women in Maasai culture typically marry very young and do not have access to the same educational opportunities as men. A girls' school was indeed attached to this particular shop; the girls made the crafts to help fund their own education. I felt slightly ashamed for brushing off the owner upon hearing this, and I vowed to give his offer more serious consideration on the return trip. After a few more laps around the various wooden sculptures, Lisa and I realized that everyone was already back on the bus, impatiently waiting for us. We jumped aboard without having time to buy anything. We were off to the Kenya–Tanzania border.

The bus soon entered what was the largest town so far. Small buildings of wood, cement, and brick packed in close to the road as we wound our way through the village. The buildings were well worn, as if the equatorial winds had been blowing through for generations. Once past the town center, we pulled into a large parking lot. It was full of diesel trucks spewing smog and mud-covered transports idling impatiently. Various safari jeeps and shuttle buses were parked in between these giant vehicles. On the far side of the lot was a little building with a faded sign: PASSPORT CONTROL. It looked more like an old farmhouse than a government office.

I'd like to say that we waited patiently in line to process our passports and legally enter Tanzania. But there were no lines to wait in, nor any clear indication of what we were supposed to do or where we were supposed to go. Luckily, Lisa and I had already taken care of our visas with the Kenyan and Tanzanian embassies in the United States. So we joined the crowd and shoved our way to the front with everyone else. We waited for the rather unhappy man behind the counter to grumble "next," and once he did, we thrust our papers in front of him. He took a brief look at our forms, stamped them, and tossed them back across the counter.

"Thank you," I said, smiling broadly, trying my new-found technique for making friends in East Africa.

"Next," he growled back. Apparently, just like elsewhere, in Africa bureaucrats are immune to smiles.

Now back on the bus for the final hour of our trip, we crossed into Tanzania and on to the town of Arusha. As we traversed the savanna, a new feature began to inhabit the expansive countryside that had mesmerized us all morning; we began to see mountains. Some were small mounds while others towered high above the vast plain. They each stood alone among the golden fields, each an individual monolith among the geological upheavals of the past.

"I think that's Kili," I said, pointing out the largest of the peaks to the south.

"Wow. It's huge," Lisa replied. "Wait," she corrected. "There's no snow on it and it doesn't have the flat top."

She was right. This particular peak had a rather pointed summit and no snow at all. It wasn't Kilimanjaro, not even close. We continued our vigil undeterred, waiting for Kilimanjaro to reveal itself and debating the potential of each new formation as it appeared. We couldn't wait to see the famous figure of Tanzania.

While we were scanning the horizon for Kilimanjaro, the gentleman in the seat in front of us was scanning the skies for a mobile phone signal. He and his wife were from the United Kingdom and appeared to be on a safari holiday. As we journeyed across the African plains and passed Maasai villages (with no evidence of even a single phone line), this man was sending text messages across the heavens to friends and family back in London.

The final destination for our coach bus—and for all the passengers except me and Lisa—was the Novatel Hotel, on the outskirts of Arusha. According to the Tanzanian Ministry of Tourism, 70 percent of the visitors who come to Tanzania use Arusha as their home base before setting out on safaris or other adventures. But Lisa and I had chosen a more adventurous path—or so we told ourselves. We were heading farther east, to the town of Moshi, at the foot of Kilimanjaro.

The hotel parking lot buzzed with activity. Various caravans, shuttles, safari jeeps, and buses filled with khaki-clad guests lugging an assortment of backpacks and duffel bags. Some were heading into Arusha to find their hotels and relax. Others were off to the wilds to start their safari. Lisa and I sat on our bags, waiting for our ride to appear.

Almost an hour passed. The last jeep had pulled out and the dust had finally settled. We had questioned multiple drivers, but all said they were not going to Moshi and just to wait. So we waited. But as we sat alone in the gravel parking lot on the outskirts of town, we began to get nervous. What if no one came? What if they'd forgotten about us? How would we get to Moshi? We'd already paid for this portion of our trip, transferring a large amount of money to a bank in Moshi. What was to prevent those people from just leaving us sitting in the parking lot?

I've traveled to many different places. In almost every trip there is a moment like this—a moment of fear and the startling realization: *I am completely at the mercy of the locals. I am naked to whatever they want to do and my only protection is the thin hope that they are basically kindhearted and willing to help a traveler in need.* In the end my optimism has always been rewarded. With more time and experience in any country, the feeling of nakedness passes and I am reminded that most people are basically good and can be relied upon to help a stranger. The particular culture simply dictates *how* this help is expressed.

In Tanzania we had not been forgotten. But time moves at a different speed there, and we soon learned that a thirty-minute delay was nothing to worry about. A car pulled into the empty lot and a short, Indian-looking man stepped out of the beat-up, yellow-brown Buick.

"Go Moshi?" he asked in uncomfortable English. Lisa and I breathed a sigh of relief.

"Yes," I replied. "We were told to wait here for the continuing shuttle to Moshi. Are you our ride?" Obviously, this went well beyond his limited English skills. Rather than respond to my questions, he smiled, grabbed our bags, and threw them into the trunk. He opened the door to the car and waved us in to the back seat. We were now testing my theory on the kindness of strangers well beyond my personal comfort level. We were alone in the middle of a foreign country, with no working knowledge of the language, being asked to jump into the car of a complete stranger, without any confirmation of who he was or what his intentions were.

So, naturally, we got in the car without objection.

We made our way into the center of bustling Arusha. The wide streets were packed with people on all sides, and carts and small shops pressed into the road. We passed large crowds of people hawking items on the sidewalk and throngs of pedestrians. The driver pulled up to three different hotels, and each time it was the same. He would smile at us and gesture for us to wait. Then he would go into the hotel and argue for a while with someone before returning to the car to drive on to the next hotel. Each time he left us, the car was immediately swarmed by young children begging and bony men selling t-shirts and other knickknacks. We had spent the morning hiding out in the world of tourists, insulated from our surroundings. Now the local realm was reaching its hand through the crack in the window and demanding our attention.

After three attempts our driver decided to give up. He explained in his broken English that there was no additional shuttle to Moshi, but if we paid him, he would take us the rest of the way.

"We already paid to get to Moshi," Lisa explained.

"No shuttle. You pay me. I take you."

"We already paid," she objected. "You need to get us to Moshi."

I was surprised and impressed with Lisa's force. Personally, I didn't feel as though we had much of a bargaining position. But she persisted and the driver abruptly ceased his objections. He started the car, maneuvered down one of the side streets, and pulled into what appeared to be the local garbage collection facility. Piles of rubbish were everywhere. Near the entrance a few women squatted along the street selling grilled corn over an open flame and warm soda under the hot sun.

Our driver stepped from the car, motioning for us to follow. Again, we obeyed without question (although with a fair amount of concern and confusion). He pulled our bags from the trunk and dragged them over to a nearby bus. It was a small, diesel commuter bus slightly larger than the tourist bus we had sat in all morning. Looking around I realized my initial assumption had been wrong: this wasn't the local dump; it was the local bus depot. Several buses were parked in a lot, with young men standing on the roofs. The seats were filling with patiently waiting passengers. We were about to experience firsthand how the locals traveled.

Without a word our driver shoved his way onto the bus and wiggled through the crowded passengers to the back. He made his way to the last seat along the back wall and began arguing with a young couple holding a small baby. They went back and forth a few times until the couple apparently relented and changed seats. Our driver shoved his way back out and indicated our accommodations were ready.

We stood in shock, not knowing what to do. Had he convinced them to move by telling of his own sorry predicament? Had he demanded they move for the rich white tourists? I tried to ask what had just happened, but our driver didn't understand a word I said. My mind raced for what to do. This was apparently our only ride to Moshi, and we had no way of discussing our concerns with him or anyone else on the bus. Our bags had been tossed to a young boy on the roof of the bus, and our driver pushed us on board, past the staring passengers, stuffing us into the now vacated seats.

"You no pay," he said. "I pay. You no pay. They ask you but you no pay." With that, he turned and left. The entire bus of black faces stared at us as we looked back, as confused as they probably were.

Our anonymous guide took off, and the bus continued to fill. We sat dumbfounded with no ideas but to just sit there. Seats were folded down to cover the aisle spaces and passengers wedged themselves into every opening possible. Children sat on the laps of strangers or stood between the legs of people with seats, and young men hung out the door. Every seat was stuffed with four to five people. Eventually, filled way beyond capacity, the bus lurched onto the street and we were off. Of course, "capacity" is a relative term. I lost count, but there were more than forty-five passengers crammed into a bus meant to accommodate only half that number.

Lisa sat on my right, relishing the experience, the chance to feel what life was really like in Tanzania. As my trepidation passed, I too began to relax. We were no longer cramped up inside the stuffy house of security. We weren't watching the world from a tourist bus any more; we were a part of it now. We had stepped out into the hot fresh air of the real Tanzania—and it was wonderful. The people packed in around us also warmed to our presence, and we soon felt as if we belonged there. Our fellow passengers were kindly returning our smiles and nods, and they took us in as just another pair of Tanzanian travelers.

The bus puttered out of Arusha and onto the one-lane highway to Moshi. Lisa closed her eyes, enjoying the cool breeze that blew through the open windows. But the breeze that was so refreshing for us was too cold for our fellow passengers, who had grown up at the equator. They reached up and closed all the windows. On my left an older man sat with a small boy standing in the gap between his legs. The gentleman was thin with gray hair, faded brown slacks, and a button-down dress shirt. He held a walking stick and his vacant eyes were fixed forward, focusing on nothing in particular. He was blind. The boy stood holding the seat in front for balance and stared forward into the void as well. His right eye was covered with mucus that had already caked his eyelid shut. He would be blind in another year, if not sooner.

Tanzania has a startlingly high rate of blindness in children resulting from a number of sources, including vitamin deficiency, washing in putrid streams, and close contact with other infected people. In all likelihood this child and his whole family would lose their sight from what appeared to be trachoma, a contagious bacterial conjunctivitis, sometimes called the "disease of the poor." Trachoma is the leading cause of preventable blindness and affects more than a hundred million people worldwide, with the vast majority being children.

I couldn't stop staring at this boy, his future so plainly written on his face. As an American, I come from the land of "anything is possible," where medicine can be bought in any small town and an eye infection is a minor nuisance. But this child's whole life could be decided by the stream he got water from or if he was lucky enough to gain access to the most basic medicine. With a sudden pang of guilt, I realized I had thrown his cure into the trash only two weeks prior. I had recently received a prescription for antibacterial eye drops but had not finished the bottle. I had cleaned out the bathroom and thrown away the remaining drops without thinking twice. My garbage could have prevented this young boy from going blind. It was a startling and uncomfortable realization that has continued to haunt me. To this day, every time I sit in a doctor's office, I wonder what happened to that boy. When I walk through the drugstore down the street and see the ready access I have to such vast quantities of routine medicines, I think of him and his family.

The bus continued, stopping every few minutes. Our comfy tourist bus had zoomed along at over sixty miles an hour, zipping past town after town. The local bus stopped at every single small building and settlement we encountered. At each stop a few people squeezed out or a few more packed in. One of the men hanging out the door would extract the appropriate fare as the bus jerked back onto the road. At one stop a young child, seemingly alone, needed a ride. I have no idea where his family was. Perhaps one of them was hanging off the door. The child was too small for that, though, and instead was handed into the bus and passed back over the heads of the passengers like a sack of potatoes. Finally, he came to rest in the lap of an older woman. He took his new seat without complaint and we were off again.

By midafternoon we pulled into the little town of Moshi, nestled just off the southern slope of Kilimanjaro. The city is estimated to be home to almost 150,000 people. However, it looked more like 2,000. People on the street greeted each other unhurriedly and small groups stood around sharing conversations and laughs.

The bus entered along one of the few paved streets in town, passing tiny shops and cement buildings with names like "Tanzanian Microfinance," "Fahari Cyber Café," "Aleem's Grocery," the disconcerting "Golden Shower" restaurant, and the very versatile "Chrital Zoo," which specialized in mountain climbing, safaris, gemstones, and curios. The name "Moshi" means "smoke," and as I hacked on the bus's diesel fumes, I suspected I knew why.

The center of town was built up between two long parallel streets, paved and smooth. Between them ran potholed pavement and beyond them the roads turned to dirt and pebble. Cement shops, with their wooden doors closed, lined the sidewalks. A dark woman wrapped in colorful blankets sat on the roadside, squatting on a sack of potatoes, an umbrella protecting her from the searing sun. Piles of oranges, bananas, potatoes, and other local fruits and vegetables lay out for sale on a well-worn tarp in front of her. But today was Sunday, a quiet day for business, and hers was one of the few enterprises open.

At a large gray cement structure designated MOSHI BUS TERMINAL, our bus pulled up to a raised island. Passengers quickly spewed out. We grabbed our backpacks and hoisted them onto our backs. Lisa turned to me with a "what's next?" expression. I had absolutely no idea. I had expected someone to meet us at the bus stop just like all those people back in Arusha. But I saw no one. Perhaps our change of transportation method had caused us to miss our next ride. Either way, we needed help.

I looked around for some kind of information booth, taxi stand, or tourist office. Nothing. Just a sea of people and chaos. I knew the name of our local outfitter, but I had no map, address, or phone number—just an email address. Here we were, in a foreign bus depot, with bags piled everywhere, animals packed onto buses or under seats, and hundreds of people speaking Swahili or other languages yelling back and forth at each other. There was no schedule board or information booth. There was no map or route numbers on display, no helpful ticket-taker or even a main clock. As the passengers collected their bags, taxi drivers swarmed in, eager for any business on such a slow day. They yelled at the crowd in Swahili and solicited fares. For me it felt like the Nairobi airport all over again.

But this time we were better prepared. With the knowing postures of experienced travelers, we ignored the shouting and looked around with hope for "our" ride. Finally, through the chaos I heard a voice yell out the familiar words: "Springlands Hotel." That was our destination!

"Do you know the Springlands Hotel?" I asked eagerly, practically jumping on the taxi driver.

"I take you, no problem," he boasted, and grabbed our bags without further discussion. He led us to a compact, black taxi and stuffed our bags into the tiny trunk. Tired and ready to end the day's journey, we squirmed into the cramped back seat and hunched over as we negotiated the rate. He fired up the engine and jostled down the bumpy paved road before veering onto a dirt street full of massive potholes. As we hit each crater, the car bounced and our heads rammed into the ceiling. He drove to the outskirts of Moshi, crossed a set of railroad tracks, and headed down another dirt road. We passed a small factory and several squat brick houses. Chickens scattered across the road as we sped by. After a few minutes we pulled up to a gray-walled complex and large black metal gate. The driver honked, the gates opened, and we proceeded into the Springlands Hotel, a tourist sanctuary on the outskirts of Moshi.

Surrounded by a ten-foot-high concrete wall, it is a private hotel solely for the use of climbing and safari customers. Inside the wall are guest rooms, a small bar (open all day long), a dining pavilion, a pool, sauna, television room, computer room, and gift shop. Guests can even get a massage, if scheduled in advance.

But all of this was too much for us to take in at this point. We had been traveling for three days now. The journey from Nairobi had been wonderful but exhausting. We paid our driver and shuffled over to the reception window, where we were warmly greeted by the smiling and aptly named Patience. She gave us a glass of juice and checked us into our room. We took a deep breath, collapsed onto our respective beds, and immediately fell asleep.

Mother cheetah in the Serengeti

4

Baboons Come In and Make Problems

Lisa and I woke from our sleep comas with a start. Strange noises had intruded into our slumber and forced us back to reality. I sat up in my bed blinking, trying to remember where I was. The soft glow of dusk flowed through the window and the room took on an orange tint. Outside I heard the repeated crackle and crunch of the noisy pebble path that ran between the buildings of the compound. It was evening and the other guests were returning from their safaris and climbs. Heavy boots gnashed the pebble walkway, announcing their return.

I rubbed my eyes and took in the sparse room. We each had a small twin bed, draped in mosquito netting. There was a tiny table between us with a lamp. A standing fan oscillated in the corner and a cut-out magazine picture adorned the wall. Outside, the evening breeze was cool and welcoming. I stood for a moment, letting it wash over me and help shake off the last remnants of sleep. In the center of the compound, dinner was being served in an open pavilion, where long tables were starting to fill up with groups of guests. We found a seat next to two young Canadian men who had just come off the mountain; they were celebrating their success with a few beers.

"Any suggestions?" Lisa asked them.

"Make sure you cut your toenails. It's a bitch coming down." The man pointed to his now black toenails.

The next morning we emerged considerably more rested and prepared to explore the little town of Moshi and our hotel. As I stepped out of our room, I was struck by my first clear view of Mount Kilimanjaro. To say the mountain was massive would be a considerable understatement. It was gigantic, enormous, humongous, and just plain very big. The huge, solitary formation dominated the entire horizon. The near side of the mountain started a few miles north, where it erupted out of the flat landscape. It gradually rose up into the clouds in a long, sloping ridge and simply disappeared. I tried to see where the far slope returned to the plains, but it was hardly visible in the distance. A thick ring of clouds draped over the top half of the mountain and shielded the summit and glaciers from view. The green forest extended from the brown base and covered the miles between us. There were no foothills or rolling meadows to gradually rise up and warn that a mountain was about to explode from the savanna. It stood alone, a majestic monolith above all of Africa. After mere seconds I was already having doubts about whether I would actually be able to climb that thing. It was very, very big.

I would have thought something that massive would have been spotted immediately by the first European traders in Africa. But it hadn't been. The first recorded sighting of the mountain comes from the journals of the sixteenth-century explorer Fernandez de Enciso, who wrote: "West of [Mombasa] stands the Ethiopian Mountain Olympus, which is exceeding[ly] high, and beyond it are the Mountains of the Moon, which are the sources of the Nile." Unfortunately for Encisco, that was all he recorded. He was not able to get close enough to the mountain to map its location and details adequately. So he doesn't get the credit for discovering Kilimanjaro.

It wasn't until a nearsighted German missionary named Johannes Rebmann penetrated the continent in the spring of 1848 that the mountain was "officially" discovered by Europeans. Rebmann and his fellow missionary and countryman Dr. Ludwig Krapf had come to East Africa in 1846 with the goal of establishing a mission near Mombasa, a growing trade community. They'd heard rumors of a peak named Kilima Njaro in the Chagga lands two hundred miles west. The stories told of a mountain covered with gold and silver and protected by evil spirits. Any who tried to climb the mountain and steal the riches were stricken down. Some brave souls were never seen again, while others came back with their limbs deformed and blackened.

Krapf and Rebmann had a vision for Africa. They wanted to set up a series of missions spanning the continent from east to west. Missionaries would spread The Word and fight the growing slave trade. This vision propelled Rebmann into the interior of the continent in 1848, in search of possible mission sites and future souls for saving. His patient and infinitely useful guide was a Muslim named Bana Kheri, who had led slave and trade caravans across the interior several times. Bana Kheri spoke many local languages, understood the various political pitfalls each culture presented, and was extremely practical.

Rebmann was, by all accounts, a good man. But he was also a foreigner in Africa and a devout Lutheran, both character traits contributing to his unusual capacity to accidentally insult his local hosts. While he found the native people "noble," he was also troubled by their naked appearance and frequently considered the tribes' "uncultivated" practices and gifts disgusting, often refusing to take part. He also refused to accept Bana Kheri's advice and arm the caravan with rifles. On one occasion Rebmann demanded that the team spend the night in a location Bana Kheri knew to be rife with bandits and native raiders. But Rebmann and Bana Kheri survived. Despite Rebmann's consistently naive judgment, they were never assaulted or attacked in any way. Bana Kheri was able to smooth over most of Rebmann's mishaps with the local chiefs and eventually broker an amiable relationship.

On the morning of May 11, 1848, Rebmann spotted a massive formation in the distance. In his diary he wrote: "I observed something remarkably white on the top of a high mountain, and first supposed that it was a very white cloud, in which supposition my guide also confirmed me; but having gone a few paces more I could no more rest satisfied with that explanation; and while I was asking my guide a second time whether that white thing was indeed a cloud, and scarcely listening to his answer that yonder was a cloud but what that white was he did not know, but supposed it was coldness, the most delightful recognition took place in my mind of an old well-known European guest of snow." Rebmann and his party continued on to the Chagga kingdom of Kilema. He was not able to make it all the way to the mountain on this trip, but he returned months later and was able to accurately describe the main attributes and location of the mountain. He later sent this information to Europe.

But news of snow at the equator was not received with the awe and enthusiasm one might expect. The leading expert on East African geography at the time was William

Desborough Cooley, who had written numerous essays about the region's geography based on such sources as Arab and Portuguese writings. He had, however, never actually *been* to East Africa. When Cooley heard of Rebmann's sighting, he wrote a snide and arrogant article in the journal *Athenaeum*: "I deny altogether the existence of snow on Mount Kilimanjaro." He had nothing but insults for both Rebmann and Krapf and appeared to make it a hobby to discredit their discovery. In the end Krapf became so disillusioned with the learned men of England that he gave up trying to convince them of the mountain's existence, declaring in *Travels and Missionary Labours*, "Let Geography perish!"

But the golden age of geography did not perish. And not all geographic thinkers of the time were as stubborn and closed-minded as Cooley had been. The French Société Geographie awarded both Rebmann and Krapf medals for their valuable contribution to the study of geography. In the end even the National Geographic Society confirmed the existence of Kilimanjaro. Rebmann and Krapf were vindicated, and Cooley was marginalized.

Lisa and I sat down for breakfast next to the Canadians we had met the night before. Alex and Dominique were currently working in South Africa on a flight simulator project with Airbus. Over cold toast and eggs they invited us to join them in town for the day. Their guide had invited them to his home, and we were welcome to tag along. "He's called 'Chief,'" Alex explained. "He's a really great guy. We loved having him as our guide."

Chief met us at the hotel, and we all packed into a beat-up yellow taxi and took off down the dirt road. We passed through the main center of Moshi, past the bus depot, and then back out the other side onto more dirt roads and past more square red-brick houses. We pulled up to Chief's home, where a small wooden cart filled with fruit for sale stood in front. The building itself was made of brown concrete, with a corrugated metal roof and built into almost a compound. In each of the building's four corners was a one-room home, and in the center was a cement courtyard with a single water spigot sticking out of the ground over a drain.

Chief led us through the compound, waving us through a curtain and into one of the single-room dwellings. "Welcome to my home," he said. A solitary lightbulb hung from the ceiling, casting a pale glow on a small couch and bed. Some clothing and a stack of papers were piled up in the corner. Chief cleared some space on the couch and we took a seat.

"How much does a place like this go for?" Dominique inquired.

"The room is about eight dollars a month, and water and electricity another two dollars."

"Hey, that's better than Toronto."

Alex and Dominique joked with Chief about their climb. After a few moments a woman appeared in the doorway with a tray of beers and a Coke. It was Chief's sister, who lived in one of the other rooms. His brothers occupied the other two rooms and the compound was theirs to share.

"Have a beer, Chief," Alex offered.

"No, thank you," he replied, sipping his soda. "My grandfather told me never to drink before 3:00 PM." Chief was a Maasai. His parents still lived the traditional way, and he would spend much of the rainy season with them back at their village while there was little tourism work. But he had made the decision to leave the traditional life after school, as so many young children do today.

Chief wanted to know more about our backgrounds. He couldn't understand that Alex and Dominique weren't from the United States.

"We're from Canada," they protested. "They're Americans. We're Canadians."

"What's the difference?" Chief asked innocently.

"Well, they're different countries," we tried. But after a few moments of muddling through this, it was clear the difference meant very little to Chief. We gave up.

"Do you have places like this in Canada?" he asked, motioning to his home. "Are people poor in Canada?"

"Some" was the only response we could muster. For Chief this just did not make sense. How was it possible for a country to be so rich that its people fly across the world for pleasure and climb a mountain, wearing clothes worth more than his annual salary? Surely if there was so much wealth in North America, there could be no poor people. It was beyond our ability to explain.

We decided to have lunch at the Leopard Hotel and took the taxi back into town. On the restaurant's roof terrace we sipped orange sodas while the boys told stories, reliving their climb. As they joked back and forth, I got more and more confused by some of the names. Finally, out of desperation, I asked: "I'm sorry, but what exactly is your name?"

"Jeff," Chief replied.

"Is that Chief or Jeff?" I poked further.

"Jeff," he answered.

The Canadians were dumbfounded. "You mean we've been calling you 'Chief' for over a week and your name is really 'Jeff'?"

"Yes," the newly identified Jeff confirmed with a forgiving smile.

After this informative lunch we strolled around downtown Moshi for a few minutes and left Jeff to return to the hotel. We gave him a small tip as a token of our appreciation and he was off. As we spoke with other climbers, we heard similar stories about home visits with guides. Some clients felt the guides' sole motivation was to solicit more tips by showing how poor their living conditions were. I never had the feeling with Jeff that he was trying to scam us or solicit anything more than information. He was clearly interested in learning more about these people he had guided and seemed open to sharing his world with us as well. Lisa and I were thrilled to get an inside look into life in Tanzania. And if culture dictated we tip Jeff for this, we were more than willing to do so.

The next morning we met our Tanzanian safari guide, Roy. He was tall and lean, and offered a soft smile as he greeted us. We climbed into his white Range Rover and headed north. As we drove out of town, the scenery began to improve. The crowded streets of Moshi gave way to the open savanna, and concrete shops were replaced by small fruit stands. The few people we saw wore Maasai blankets or colorful wraps instead of shirts and slacks. Crowded mini-buses were replaced by people walking or bicycles piled high with water bottles.

We drove for hours, becoming drowsy in the hot sun and dry dust. The countryside and small towns rolled by, each with its own distinct personality and composition. Some were just a few mud huts with thatched roofs for protection. Other towns were larger, with wooden buildings and even a small shop with half-empty shelves of cans and boxes. From time to time we'd pass a school, a larger wood building that looked as though the British had built it. The schools were painted white with iconic clock towers in the middle, classrooms extending off to both sides, and a playground out front. But we rarely saw any children at play there.

After several hours we reached the gates of Lake Manyara National Park, famous for its pink flamingos and tree-climbing lions. Roy pulled into the visitor center and suggested we take a break. He stepped out, popped open the top of the Range Rover, and raised it three feet. When we climbed back in, we could easily stand, looking out the top of the jeep in any direction while having ample shade from the hot sun. As the jeep crept through the gate, we stood with our heads out the open top, gaping at our surroundings and peering deep into the forest in the hopes of spotting something spectacular.

It didn't take long. We pulled into a pack of baboons and were beside ourselves with excitement. Our first real wildlife! "Baboons!" we cried.

"Baboons," Roy confirmed.

They sat in the dirt on the side of the road, grooming each other, gnawing on various twigs, and actually posing while I snapped far too many photos. Eventually the thrill wore off and we were ready to hunt bigger quarry. We found a mother and baby elephant marching through a meadow, pulling up grass with their trunks and stuffing it in their mouths. Giraffes stood nearby, ripping thorny acacia branches off with their tough tongues. At each stop we stood in awe of the animals and our amazing proximity to them. We were mere yards away, watching them in their natural environment.

We meandered along the windy park road, coming to a bend where the forest cleared before Lake Manyara. A herd of zebra munched on grass as a nearby group of wildebeests made its way to the water's edge. In the distance the deep blue waters turned to pink, transformed by millions of flamingos. We stopped at the water's edge and got out of the jeep to stretch our legs and get a better look.

"This is amazing," Lisa whispered, as if the slightest noise might disturb the serenity around us. But within five minutes seven more jeeps pulled up and piles of noisy tourists poured out, snapping pictures and chattering about how pretty everything was.

We were tired and it was time to go. Roy drove us out of the park and up the side of the great Rift Wall to our hotel, the Lake Manyara Lodge. It was perched overlooking the park and the lake, and we could see across the valley for miles.

"I will meet you at nine tomorrow morning," Roy announced. I was shocked. We had spent the whole day with Roy, and he had been a wonderful travel companion. He had shared Tanzania with us and I was looking forward to learning more from him over dinner. But that's not the way it works, and he went to stay at a different hotel in town—"a local hotel," he called it.

The bellman greeted us and took us to our room. "Please close your windows when you leave the room to prevent problems," he said.

"What kind of problems?" I asked.

"Baboons come in and make problems."

We had booked our safari to stay at "standard lodges," about the equivalent of a three-star hotel in the United States. The amenities at the Lake Manyara Lodge were sparse, but it was comfortable. If we wanted anything cheaper, we would have been sleeping in a tent, something we weren't ready to do since we'd soon be spending seven days in a tent on the mountain.

As we entered the dining room for dinner, my first thought was that we were underdressed. Lisa and I both wore the khaki pants, t-shirts, and sandals we'd been wearing all day in the jeep. It was clear, however, that dinner was a more formal affair than that. Almost all of the guests were wearing dresses and high heels or slacks and dress shirts. The occasion apparently called for smart-casual, and we just hadn't gotten the memo. We also appeared to be the only Americans, as German and British accents filled the room.

My second realization was that, after a day of freely roaming the countryside with Roy, we had returned to tourist East Africa. Looking around the room, I was struck by the fact that all of the guests were white European, and all of the staff were black. It shouldn't have come as a shock; we were in Tanzania after all. But having spent the past few years in New York and California, where there is no ethnic majority and groups mingle freely, it surprised me to see such a glaring divide. Jeff and Roy were skilled guides and I had felt like their guest. Now we were back to "white tourist land" with black people serving us. The abrupt shift felt awkward to me.

The next morning the soft red glow of the early dawn crept into our room through the east-facing window. Jet lag still woke us early, so we went out to the balcony to watch the sunrise. We had a perfect view over Lake Manyara as life began to emerge. In the half-light large herds of elephants, zebras, wildebeests, and giraffes made their way from the safety of the forest across the open plains. As they approached the water, the herds spread out and intermixed. From above we watched the various colors, sizes, and shapes mingling on the green field. The flamingos came alive, and small flocks took off from the calm blue water. We sat for an hour watching from our safe perch.

"I hate to be so 'Disney,' but you really can see the circle of life," Lisa said. "It's just amazing. I can't believe we're actually here."

Roy met us punctually at 9:00 and we headed up into the fertile highlands of the Ngorongoro Crater Conservation Area. The dry savanna slowly changed to lush green countryside, and the acacia trees were joined by manyara, wild mango, and fig trees. Bulging bushes overflowed onto the road and grassy hills rolled out in every direction. It was in complete contrast to the arid environment we had seen all day prior. By the time we peaked at over 7,000 feet on the rim of the Ngorongoro Crater, the temperature had dropped into the fifties. Although we were only two degrees south of the equator, we actually began to shiver. It was the first time we'd been cold since arriving in Africa.

As we came down the other side of the crater, the trees disappeared again and only the green grasses of the savanna remained. We shot down the dirt road, far from civilization. The road curved sharply through the tall grass and as we came around a bend, we discovered four young boys standing on the shoulder. Their faces were decorated with white markings; they wore dark baggy garments and carried small herding sticks.

Roy slowed the vehicle. "They have just completed their circumcision," he explained. "After they are circumcised, they must live apart from the village for a while." Circumcision is a major event in a young Maasai male's life. It's a rite of passage and a test of his strength and will. When the holy man cuts off the young man's foreskin, he must endure it like a warrior. He must not shout out in pain or try to kick the knife away. To do so would show unacceptable weakness and would embarrass both the boy and his family.

These industrious young men had added a new trick to the old ritual. To make a good thing out of a, shall we say, bad experience, they hung out by the side of the road, hoping to attract tourists willing to pay to take a picture of them. I always struggle with these choices. On the one hand, the boys were enterprising and probably should be paid for their time and trouble if I wanted to take a picture. On the other hand, I've seen entire cultures decimated by this kind of tourism. I once visited a small village in Thailand where tourists could come and see the lifestyle of "real" hill people. But after years of being paid for photos, the men and women no longer worked in the fields or repaired their dilapidated homes. They just squatted by the side of the road smoking opium and waiting for tourists to come and pay them for pictures. The entire economy and way of life had been destroyed by people like me who probably just wanted to learn more about a different culture.

In Thailand I had to walk away. It was too sad to see the once proud people turned into beggars. I took no photos there. But these soon-to-be Maasai warriors didn't seem like beggars to me, they seemed brave and entrepreneurial. So I gave in to my inner tourist, snapped one photo, and paid the young men one U.S. dollar for it. I didn't like the idea of paying for a picture, but after knowing what they'd been through, I couldn't help myself.

The road curved around the side of the crater and to the north; the whole savanna opened up before us. We could

see miles of rolling hills and wide open space with acacia trees spread out across the landscape. On the sloping
green fields below us was a Maasai village. A ring fence
of wood and bushes had been constructed around a group
of small huts. Each hut was a round, one-room structure
made of brown dirt and mud with a thatched roof. Goats
and chickens roamed freely within the fence as women
worked and children played.

Maasai culture is fascinating and amazingly paternal-
istic. The huts I was looking at were actually built by the
women. When a man takes a wife, a decision she has no
part in, she must build her own house out of dung and mud.
The Maasai are polygamous and the husband can move
from house to house to any of his wives. Each wife will
live with her own offspring and vie for their best interests
as a part of the family unit. One of the main things a wife
will try to get for her children is cattle. The entire Maasai
economic structure revolves around cattle. The size of a
herd dictates the wealth of a man. I say "man" because
women aren't given cattle. When a man takes a wife, he
pays her family for her in cattle (usually around fifty), and
she is allocated a portion of the herd to help care for. This
allocation is the basis for what will later be handed over to
her son. Young girls don't get cattle directly.

A man's job is to manage and protect the cattle. Lions
can snatch a wife, but for heaven's sake, don't let them
take the cattle. Young boys are put to work with the herds
almost from birth. They start by helping with the goats
and eventually graduate to the real herd. While this may
seem unfair to some, there are reasons for it. The health
of the cattle dictates the health of the family. The Maasai
diet consists mainly of milk mixed with blood and some
occasional meat. If the cows go, all the food goes. And
the cows have a precarious existence, vulnerable to the

weather and any number of predators. Aside from lions, countless scavengers, including hyenas, would love to have a nice juicy steak. Another major predator is other Maasai. When times get lean, the Maasai don't degrade themselves by eating grains and other such foods. The gods gave the great Maasai cattle and that's what they eat. If theirs are gone, then they might steal some from another tribe.

Once past the village, we entered the Serengeti Plain. The rolling green hills were behind us now, and the landscape flattened to the expanding savanna, the grasses parched by the hot sun. On top of a small hill to the west stood a pair of ostrich, male and female. They looked up at us as we passed, gave a sneer, and went back to picking at the dry grass with their beaks.

One of the things that makes the Serengeti so amazing is the annual wildebeest migration. More than 1.5 million animals make a circuit around the Maasai Mara of Kenya and the Serengeti of Tanzania. This time of year, September, the Serengeti was dry and depleted, driving the migration north into the more fertile Maasai Mara. Once the long rainy season comes to Tanzania in October and November, the vegetation will come to life again and the migration will move south into the Serengeti to live off the lush green grasses. As the area dries out in June and July, the migration will again make its way north for better feeding.

Imagine the entire populations of Houston, or Philadelphia, or the San Francisco Bay Area, including San Jose, all just standing around eating grass and minding their own business. Imagine this cloud of people quietly wandering in a massive circle around the state of Connecticut. That's what the migration is like. It is also the largest mobile buffet on the planet. Many of the predators in the region depend on the migration for food. Thousands of wildebeests die every year as they circuit the savanna. But not all are picked off by ravaging lions. It is estimated that about 70 percent of the meat consumed from the migration is not killed but actually found. The weaker animals, unable to keep up, fall and die along the journey while the strong keep moving.

Because the migration was to the north as we entered the park, we had to look a bit harder to find wildlife. But it didn't take Roy's finely trained senses long to find something spectacular for us to see. He veered off the road toward a large set of boulders. We scanned the tall brown grass and squat brush. We peered into the small cracks in the rocks, looking for some sign of life. After a few minutes we spotted a female cheetah crouched under a bush on the far side of the rocks. I had seen a cheetah in a zoo, but this was radically different. Her long legs held her lean body tall, perched above the dry grass. Her eyes darted from spot to spot as she scanned the horizon. She wasn't lazing in the sun or sitting bored, waiting to be fed. She was a coiled spring of power and we marveled at her lanky beauty for almost an hour.

We sat transfixed, and two other jeeps pulled up to see what we were looking at. Several heads popped up onto the top of the jeeps with large cameras hiding their faces. "Wow, cool," someone said. Several snapped a few pictures and then the two jeeps drove off.

But we couldn't leave. We were mesmerized by so much power and speed compacted in the lean, fuzzy frame. Our patience did not go unrewarded. Finally, after forty-five minutes of sitting quietly, the cheetah paid us for our time. From the thicket behind her, four small cubs slowly appeared. The little fur balls romped and tugged at their mother, grabbing her ear, pulling her whiskers, and shoving her body to get at some milk. All the while she maintained her vigil across the open plains.

We pulled away to give her back her privacy and to search for more animals. Roy stayed off the main road, going cross-country and searching out various water holes he knew. After a few attempts he found a pride of more than ten lions lazing in the sun by a small pond. Nearby, a group of gazelle sipped cautiously at the edge of the water. We stood in the jeep, peering over the top, while Roy gave us a lesson on lions. It turns out the male lion is not really that different from his counterparts in other species. He sleeps all day and does as little work as possible. The female does all the hunting, and even then the male gets to eat first. His jobs are reproduction and security. Since the vast majority of the lions' diet is protein, they spend more than twenty hours a day sleeping and digesting. They are typically active at night, but only for a short period of time.

It was midafternoon and these lions showed no interest in doing anything but lying in the grass and stretching out for a nap. But even relaxed, they were impressive. Their lean, muscular bodies exuded power and royalty. It was obvious why they are called the King of the Beasts.

"Shouldn't those gazelle be a little more concerned?" Lisa asked, pointing to the nearby herd. "The lions are right there."

"Lions are lazy," Roy explained. "They will not chase anything if it is more than thirty yards away."

As if to prove Roy's point, one of the lionesses stood, stretched, and slowly sauntered over to the pond. The small gazelle herd was immediately on alert, eyes darting toward the lioness, heads and tails popping up in alarm. But they didn't run. They continued to drink, with one eye now fixed on the lioness. As she got closer to the water, she noticed one careless young gazelle that clearly didn't fear her enough. Suddenly her relaxed frame tightened and her shoulder blades flexed as she crouched into a hunter's stance. She slowly stalked her prey, slithering through the tall grass. But the gazelle had noticed her and finally began to show the proper respect. Gingerly, it moved outside the lioness's thirty-yard zone. The lioness sprang from the grass and trotted half-heartedly to chase the gazelle. Reminded who was boss, the gazelle sprinted, and the small herd ran a hundred yards away. The lioness sat down to drink at the water's edge, as if nothing had happened.

Roy had considerable knowledge of lions. In fact, he knew a lot about almost everything we saw. He shared it in regular but bite-sized portions so as not to overwhelm us. While we were watching the cheetah earlier in the day, Roy had explained how the black marking across a cheetah's eyes prevents glare from the sun. Cheetahs hunt with speed, and keen eyesight is required to spot their prey and track it at high velocity. He discussed the female cheetah's hunting and mating habits, her preferred prey, and other anecdotal tidbits.

Roy was an interesting study in much of what was working in Tanzania. He had scrimped and saved for years to fund his own training to become a safari guide. He'd then spent a year learning his new profession while living off his meager savings. Now, having secured a good job and salary by Tanzanian standards, he continued to advance himself. He was at a time in his career when he could coast and impress clients with his wit and humor rather than study further. He later told us he had never been that close to cheetahs before; it was evident he had enjoyed the experience as much as we had. We were enjoying our time with Roy, exploring the Serengeti with him. It didn't feel like we were tourists who were paying a guide for a service. He was an equal—in fact, a superior. He was our teacher and lecturer, and our respect for him grew the more he shared with us and the more we learned about him.

Our final stop for the day was the hippo pool. Roy took us up a remote dirt stretch and parked among the scrub. "It's okay. You can get out here," he reassured us. After seeing the lions, we were a bit hesitant but agreed and followed him. He led us through the brush along a dirt road to the edge of a dried-up pond.

"Hippo pond," Roy said, pointing at the parched hole in front of us.

I looked into the cracked dirt hole and did not see any hippos. I stepped out onto a rock outcropping that extended into what was once water. I had taken only a few steps when suddenly a gray flash emerged to my left. All I saw was two massive spiked teeth as a huge gray mass lunged and snarled at me. Its enormous jaw snapped. I leaped out of my sandals as Roy chuckled at my reaction. The hippo, as it turns out, was a safe fifteen feet away and merely protesting our disturbance.

"Hippos are very aggressive," Roy stated in his deadpan way.

As my heartbeat slowly returned to normal, I got a better view of my attacker. It was a huge hippo, about eight feet long and almost as wide, stewing in the last puddle of water left. He had just enough room to stand but not enough to move. It was a small, pathetic pond being defended to the death by a very aggressive tenant.

"The hippo must leave," Roy quietly opined.

"How?" I asked.

"At night, the hippos get out and walk. It is very hard, but they do it. The hippo can go to another hole with more water," Roy explained. "But I think this one is stubborn."

The best time to see wild animals is at dawn and dusk, when they are most active in the cool, soft light of the day. At Roy's suggestion we met him at seven the next morning for a different view of the Serengeti wildlife. As the sun climbed over the eastern horizon, it bathed the landscape of acacia and burnt grass in hues of golden red. The air was cool and refreshing as Lisa and I peeked over the top of the jeep.

Roy brought us to the edge of a small creek and we spotted three lionesses on the prowl. They strode along the creek's edge, eyes scanning the grass and brush, all of their senses activated and alert. They marched single file, one after the other, about fifty feet apart. As each one approached the jeep, I could feel the tension in her muscles and the raw power in her legs. The third lioness was about to pass when she caught the scent of a nearby solitary gazelle. Immediately her body coiled under her powerful legs and she hunched into the tall grass, almost disappearing. She stalked in silence and slowly advanced upon her intended prey. This wasn't a mission to scare off a disrespectful gazelle—this was for breakfast. Her body slithered through the brush and with each careful step her shoulder blades flexed along her back. The lioness advanced to within forty feet when the gazelle's head shot up and its nose twitched. It glanced in the direction of the lioness and sprinted away. As it bolted, the lioness sprang forward in a last-ditch effort, but the gazelle was too far away and too fast. The lioness gave up and slowly returned to hunt with the rest of the pride.

We spent that night at the Ngorongoro Wildlife Lodge, perched on the crater rim at 7,300 feet above sea level. The deck offered expansive views into the crater, with its flowing fields of grass, small forests of acacia trees, and a dried lakebed awaiting the seasonal rains. The air was cool and the setting sun transformed the sky from blue to purple to red and finally to pink.

At dinner we sat next to a young couple. Claude was originally from France and Jen from China. They lived together in Seattle and had just completed their Kilimanjaro climb. "We climbed the Machame Route," Jen explained. "It was great until the fourth day, when it started to rain." She was petite and soft spoken, but her tone conveyed a deep enthusiasm for her experience.

Claude seemed to be more demure about it. "I had to turn back," he stated flatly. "I had a terrible headache and just couldn't continue."

"How far did you get?" I inquired as delicately as possible.

"13,080 feet," he replied.

That wasn't very high, I thought.

"We both took Diamox," Jen added. Diamox was designed to treat glaucoma, but many climbers have found it useful in fighting altitude sickness.

"How did you do?" I probed. I had heard that a larger percentage of women summit than men because they are more "mentally tough."

"Oh, I made it," she replied without any flair. "I didn't have any problems."

◎   ◎

The next morning we joined Roy for a trip into the crater. The tall grass was parched and the only green left was in a small stand of acacia trees clustered in the far corner of the crater floor. The dry lakebed had left a large white alkaline stain with only a few smaller watering holes remaining. It didn't take long in this enclosed ecosystem to come across a pride of lions. But they weren't difficult to spot this time. We were the fifth jeep to show up, and within minutes even more had swarmed in. At the center of this circus were a male, three lionesses, and three juveniles.

The day before, the lioness had not taken any notice of us as she hunted gazelle by the creek bed. In Ngorongoro Crater it appeared that jeeps were so common, they'd almost become part of the natural ecosystem, a source of shade just like anything else. By the time we arrived, the pride had moved from their original location in the tall grass to right next to, and even under, one of the jeeps. One lioness was stretched out under the engine while the male and two other females lay in the shade next to the driver-side tires. It is illegal for a driver to move in such situations, so the tour group had become part of the show. They couldn't leave until the lions did.

As time wore on, one passenger got more impatient and bolder. She stuck her head out the window and looked at the lioness right below her. Her blond curls flopped down as she smiled at the wild huntress lounging only two feet away. It would have been nothing for that lioness to reach up with her massive paw and rip the woman out of the car. I knew lions don't typically hunt during the day, but I had to wonder if easy prey like this might just be too much to pass up.

Roy shook his head at the other guide. "He should tell her not to do that."

Seeing all the jeeps crowded around one small pride made me feel like a tourist again. We were at the wildlife theme park gawking at the animals. It was a safari rubber-necker, a traffic jam of the worst sort in the most beautiful of countries.

"We can go," Lisa told Roy.

He started the engine and slowly wove through the throng of jeeps. We were on a mission of our own. Ngorongoro Crater is one of the few places where tourists can actually see rhinos. There are some rhinos in the Serengeti, but Roy informed us the rhinos there were under armed guard to protect them from poachers. We were making our last crossing of the crater when Roy's sharp eyes spotted our quarry about 200 yards away and closing.

"There." He stopped the car and pointed out his window to the east. We scanned the distance and strained to follow his lead. Finally, we saw it: a small tank of a figure marching across the open crater floor. Lisa and I stood and looked out from the top of the jeep, focusing our binoculars and cameras. The rhino slowly approached and we waited patiently for a clear view.

"Why do poachers hunt the rhinos?" I asked Roy.

"For their horns," he replied. "They're an aphrodisiac."

It took me a moment to translate his pronunciation of the word "aphrodisiac." Discerning his meaning, I was confused. As this grumpy, stout creature advanced on our position without grace or beauty, I could see no clear connection between its armor hide and sex.

"Rhinos mate for thirty minutes," Roy explained.

"Ahh," was all I could muster.

"That might do it," Lisa agreed.

I looked back at the rhino with newfound respect. While we were discussing the rhino's sex life, he stopped his advance. He was now about fifty yards away and standing impatiently, his glare directly fixed on us. He had been trekking across the plain in a straight line when we had spotted him and pulled into his path.

"Rhinos are very aggressive," Roy said with a healthy amount of respect. "They charge cars."

"Why would they charge a car?" I asked.

"They are very territorial. They don't like to be bothered."

"Is this his territory?"

"Fifty meters," Roy replied.

"What do you mean?"

"Rhinos charge if you get closer than fifty meters." It was then that I realized that Roy had never shut off the engine. Typically when we stopped to look at something, Roy immediately shut the engine off to conserve gas and allow for a quiet view. He had not done so this time. In fact, he currently had both hands on the steering wheel and one foot on the clutch, ready for action.

I looked back at the rhino and quickly recalculated the distance. I couldn't be sure, but we must have been pretty close to his fifty-meter charge perimeter. Lisa and I looked at Roy. "We're about fifty meters now, aren't we?" I asked.

Roy looked up at us to be sure we were satisfied and appreciated the risk we were taking. Then he pulled ahead slowly. But in the end it wasn't necessary. After glaring at us long enough, the rhino decided it was more menacing to flop down on the ground and go to sleep.

Mission accomplished. We had seen the rare rhino and lived to tell the tale. That was our last great sighting, and it was time to head back to Moshi and prepare for the climb. On our four-day safari my heart and soul leaped at the sight of these amazing creatures. I was touched by their raw beauty and witnessing the circle of life playing out on the East African plain.

Bumping down the dirt road, my legs and butt ached. We had sat for two days on a plane, one day on a bus from Nairobi, and now four days in a jeep. We had hoped that a few extra days to adjust to the time zone and the additional elevation of the parks (the Ngorongoro Lodge is at

7,300 feet above sea level) might help us with the climb. It was a desperate attempt, but we would take all the help we could get. Now my muscles were screaming for action. I needed to walk. I needed motion. I loved the safari, but I'd spent six months planning and training for the climb. The safari was the bonus. Perhaps, like many climbers, we should have done the safari after the climb. Then we could have enjoyed it without having the mountain looming over us like a specter of great battles to come.

Now it was time for the mountain. No more resting and recovering. The parks were already starting to fade away in my mind as I reached forward to tomorrow's challenge. As we approached Moshi, the sun was setting and the clouds opened up before the great mountain in the distance. Tomorrow we would face Kilimanjaro.

Ascending via the Machame Route *(Photograph by Casey Lary)*

5

Polepole

Roy dropped us off back at the hotel in plenty of time for dinner, back to the long tables lined with climbers and fellow adventurers. I noticed a man across from us who had started his climb the same morning we left for our safari. Four days was not nearly enough time to summit and return. I eavesdropped on his conversation and learned that altitude sickness had forced him to turn back. He sat at the table with his shoulders slumped, face long, and body deflated; his partner was still on the mountain, continuing his adventure.

After dinner Patience, who staffed the hotel's front desk, held her nightly briefing for climbers. In her soft, smooth voice she carefully explained how to succeed on the climb. "The two most important things to remember are that you must drink a lot of water and go slowly," she said. "Very slowly. You cannot go too slow."

"I'll test that theory," Lisa whispered, reminding me of her slow-and-steady pace climbing Mount Shasta.

"*Polepole*," said Patience, pointing her finger at us to reinforce her message. A chorus of *polepole*, meaning "slowly" in Swahili, came from the staff members clearing the tables. It was a term we would hear repeatedly for the next week.

By 9:00 the next morning it was time to go. A total of eight clients were climbing the Machame Route and we were broken into three groups, each group with its own guide. There were a family of three Canadians, a German couple, and Christian, Lisa, and me. Christian worked for a Danish travel agency that had partnered with our outfitter. He was there to evaluate the climb. If all went well, he would bring tour groups from Denmark and help the local guides lead them on the mountain. Christian was a welcome addition. He was conversant in Swahili and appreciated the Tanzanian culture.

"The people are great," he beamed. "I really enjoy joking with them and teasing them. They love to laugh." Then Christian wandered off to tease and joke with another Tanzanian just to demonstrate his point.

The three of us were assigned Mohamed as our guide. He was older than most of the guides and didn't smile as much as many of the other Tanzanians we had encountered. He looked at us with deep, penetrating eyes and had the presence of a man who had climbed the mountain many times and knew what to do. I felt safe with Mohamed, if a bit intimidated.

Our diesel bus coughed out of the hotel driveway and down the road as small children waved and yelled "*mzunga!*" ("white people") at us. We headed north out of Moshi, parallel to the mountain. All morning it had been there, a massive presence. When we had risen earlier that day, I had seen the giant sentinel in the morning light. The flat top glistened with glaciers that drizzled over the summit, clinging to a past glory when they once dominated the entire peak with ice. The gray bulk of Kilimanjaro extended for miles in every direction, gradually sloping downward but still towering over the vast landscape. Thick green rain forest circled the lower flanks of the mountain, creeping up the sides before trailing off as it reached the cold, thin air. By 10:00 AM the upper mountain was completely shrouded in dense clouds.

We drove directly toward its hidden mass, eventually pulling into Machame Village at the base of the mountain. A cow stood next to us, chewing her cud in the tiny village courtyard, ringed by small, one-room cement structures with thatched roofs. On the other side of us was a cement building with three large cattle carcasses and several cuts of meat of various origins hanging in the window attracting flies. A large machete lay on the cement counter, bloody and waiting to be used. This was the town butcher. There was no refrigeration, no sanitation, and the only window was a hole in the wall.

As I looked around, I thought of how this place must have looked when the German missionary Johannes Rebmann had first arrived. He came to the kingdom of Machame on January 7, 1849. He described single-room huts nestled alongside banana fields, similar to those I was looking at. By the time of his arrival, Rebmann had become more comfortable with some of the tribal initiation rituals. At Kilema, for example, the tribesmen slaughtered a lamb, cut a ring from its head, and offered it to Rebmann as a sign of friendship. Rebmann took the ring and put it on his middle finger, accepting their friendship. He reciprocated the gesture, giving the ring to the local king, who then placed it on his own finger. They were now friends. In Machame the king, Mamkinga, splattered the missionary with blood, herbs, and the contents of a goat's stomach to signify that they were blood brothers. Welcome to the family.

While Rebmann was in Machame, he attempted to climb Kilimanjaro via what is now known as the Machame Route. Rebmann wrote to his superiors that he was able to get "so close to the snowline that, supposing no impassable abyss to intervene, I could have reached it in three or four hours." Unfortunately, that was as far as he got. It was my earnest hope that we would do better.

We pulled up a little farther and then went through the Machame Gate. Stepping off the bus, we realized that we were surrounded by hundreds of men, all of whom seemed to be staring directly at us. Dressed in well-worn clothes, they loitered by the fence, leaned against trees, and sat in the shade, waiting. They had come for work. Portering is now big business in Tanzania, requiring no formal training or education. A strong man who climbs once a month can earn more in a year than a teacher.

An estimated thirty thousand people attempt to climb Kilimanjaro every year. Most will have at least two porters, while those climbing with a more high-end outfitter might have as many as four or five. The old and young men gathered inside the Machame Gate were hoping to be hired as porters for one of the wealthy white climbers who daily arrived by the busload. In general, I have never felt very wealthy. I've always thought of myself as middle class at best. But I had a regular job, and our apartment had a shower, running water, and plenty of electricity. Relatively speaking, Lisa and I were loaded.

Our porters had the job of carrying our personal bags as well as the communal equipment and food. I watched them, dumbfounded. There were piles of fresh fruits, loaves of bread, cartons of fresh eggs, cans of coffee, and jars of honey, jam, and sugar—but no small plastic bags or lightweight containers, no "backpacking food" of any kind to reduce the load. A porter would stuff a giant basket with large jars of honey or jam, melons, oranges, and bananas, and top it off with a carton of eggs and a few loaves of bread. He would then tie the basket handles shut, balance the whole bundle on his head, and start up the mountain. In addition to the load on his head, each porter wore a small backpack, presumably carrying his own clothes. Dangling from the pack would be more items, such as several yellow gallon jugs, secured with small bits of twine.

Officially porters should carry only up to sixty pounds. But on average a porter will likely carry between sixty and eighty pounds on his head and back. Climbers are asked to keep their bags under thirty pounds and are expected to pay more if they go over. I had weighed my pack several times before leaving the States and was squeaking in at twenty-nine. A hanging scale was hoisted on a crossbeam at the trailhead, but I never saw anything, including my own pack, get weighed.

However, all of this was a big improvement over the early climbs of Rebmann's day. It wasn't long after he'd discovered Kilimanjaro that streams of Europeans rushed to Tanzania to conquer it, much to the dismay of the local people. Their leaders, who had hoped to garner more gifts from their new white visitors, frequently pressed the tribesmen into service. But hypothermia and frostbite were not experiences the half-naked natives appreciated. Frequently the porters would abandon their guests after only one day in the cold temperatures, leaving their loads on the mountain and rushing back to their warm villages below. Aside from the cold, the porters also had a healthy fear of attack from other tribes. The various kingdoms on the slopes of Kilimanjaro were frequently at war with one another. A lumbering band of warriors carrying heavy loads up the mountain was an easy target. In fact, when Rebmann met the king of Kilema, one of the king's first questions was if Rebmann's "magic book" (the Bible) could make the lions attack his hated enemies in the nearby Marangu domain. Marching into cold, dangerous territory to climb a mountain just "because it's there" (as British climber George Mallory famously put it) was not very high on the local population's list.

We strapped on our small daypacks, which contained a few liters of water, lunch that had been given to us by Mohamed, shell jackets and pants, and anything else we felt was needed for the day. Mohamed marched us to the trailhead and pushed us up the hill ahead of him. "Just walk," he ordered. "I will catch up."

A porter was trying to heft a massive basket on his head and struggled to balance the load and walk at the same time. Mohamed grabbed the basket handles and began to walk up the trail, pulling the stumbling porter behind him as he tried desperately to steady the load and keep up. Eventually the porter gained enough control for Mohamed to release him up the trail. He continued on as Mohamed went back down to usher others up the mountain. I later learned the young porter was Mohamed's little brother Juma.

The trail was wide enough to walk side by side and the slope was gentle. We were surrounded by dense rain forest, but random shafts of sunlight managed to penetrate the thick foliage, casting small patterns of light along the trail. We followed Juma and attempted to keep a slow, steady pace. It was hard to keep our enthusiasm in check, though, and our speed crept up along the relatively easy trail.

Juma looked over at me with a wry smile. "*Polepole*," he reminded me, and marched on.

Trekking up the side of the mountain, Lisa and I tried to use the time to get acquainted with our fellow travelers. The two Germans, Matthias and Suzanne, were clearly the most experienced alpinists of the group. They were decked out in all the best North Face clothing and packs. I later learned that Matthias had climbed Denali in Alaska. Both he and Suzanne were avid climbers in the Alps near their home, and they had even done some climbing in the Himalayas. At the moment they were striking out ahead of all of us. *Polepole* was not yet in their vocabulary. Their German genes called upon centuries of alpinism, propelling them up the mountain. It was clear, even at the beginning of the first day, that their advanced pace would continue for the rest of the climb.

I contented myself with trying to keep up with the Canadian family. John, the father and ringleader, was in his late sixties. He was climbing with his son, Chris, and daughter, Cecelia. Chris was a cool rebel who spent his winters working at Whistler ski resort in British Columbia; Cecelia worked for a large telecom company in Canada. John's wife had died only nine months earlier. She had been a nurse in Zambia many years ago, and John decided to take the family to Africa as a kind of memorial to her. Zambia was too dangerous at this time because of the high AIDS rate and poverty, so they hit upon climbing Kilimanjaro as an alternative. Sticking together for the most part, the three climbed quietly. John shared all of this with me while Chris was off trying to teach the porters swear words in English.

Christian caught up with us after chatting with the porters at the start of the climb. He was grinning from ear to ear at the sheer pleasure of just being here. He had been an aid worker in Tanzania a few years ago, during which time he'd learned Swahili and had come to adore the people and culture.

As we were hiking, a diminutive porter slowly caught us, carrying my tall backpack on his head. My pack was bigger than he was and teetered on top of his skull, forming a giant T as he stumbled up the trail. But that hadn't prevented him from loading it up more. On top of my pack he had strapped another small daypack. On his back was his own small pack with some food hanging off it. This was Mik, my official porter. He was also a cousin to our guide, Mohamed.

"*Polepole*," he smiled at us, panting under his load.

"*Haraka, haraka, haina baraka*," Christian replied. Mik exploded into laughter, almost dropping his carefully balanced load.

"What did you say?" I asked.

"*Haraka, haraka, haina baraka*," Christian slowly repeated. "It's a bit hard to directly translate but means something like 'there is no blessing for being faster.'"

This, to me, was Africa in one sentence. We had been on the continent for only a week and already it was clear that speed was not something valued. *Haraka, haraka, haina baraka*. I wrote this new gem in my notebook and assaulted every passing porter with it. Each time I was rewarded with a hearty laugh at the irony of the expression. Here the porters were telling us to go slowly while they rushed past us up the mountain to set up our camp before our arrival. The uptight white people were going slowly, and the relaxed Tanzanians were hurrying up the mountain.

As we ascended deeper into rain forest, the ground developed a thin layer of greasy mud on top of the hard earth beneath. It became very slippery and my boots skidded out from under me. The porters, though, were well practiced and seemed to have no trouble with the change in conditions. When we reached 8,200 feet, Lisa, the Canadian family, Christian, and I decided to take a lunch break. From our daypacks we withdrew the food Mohamed had supplied: a piece of chicken, an egg, a small cheese sandwich, an orange, a piece of chocolate, and a juice drink. We would become very familiar with this fare—it would be our lunch menu for the rest of the climb. We had enjoyed this same meal for the four days while on safari. Variety, it appeared, was not the spice of life here—chicken was.

While I gnawed on my chicken leg, the afternoon fog descended the mountain and enveloped us. The temperature dropped, the sun disappeared, and within minutes we were deep inside the same clouds I had seen from the plains below.

After organizing the porters, Mohamed had finally caught up with us. He greeted us with a "Hello," to which Chris replied, "*Jambo.*"

Mohamed smiled and returned the greeting. The official Swahili greeting is "*hu jambo*" and the reply is "*si jambo,*" which basically means "what's up?" and "not much." The tourist version was simply "*jambo.*" All over Tanzania one could hear tourists greeting guides, porters, and anyone on the street with a smile, a wave, and "*jambo.*"

"How are you?" Mohamed asked the group as we sat on our logs finishing our lunches.

"Good," was the general reply.

"Good. No problems?"

"Nope, no problems," Lisa replied as he looked in her direction.

"Good." Mohamed, we were learning, was a man of few words. He stood over us with his pack on, watching us enjoy our lunch before we set off again. The next few hours were tougher. The trail got steeper and narrower. The rains had washed away sections of dirt exposing snarled roots across the path. With each step I had to be ever more careful, negotiating the many roots that now tangled the way. I was finding my trekking poles invaluable as I gingerly made my way through the web of vines and traps.

As the afternoon waned, the group spread out along the trail. Christian and Lisa hiked behind me with Mohamed while the Canadians were in front. The Germans were well ahead of all of us. I was alone with my thoughts, wandering through a rain forest in Tanzania on the side of the greatest mountain on the continent. Giant ferns covered the damp ground while tall palm, fig, and podocarpus trees rose above them, blocking out the light. Vines and Old Man's Beard lichen hung from the tree branches, giving the forest an almost haunted feel. In the deep, dense green all around me, I could hear the many unseen birds that roosted in the dense forest rooftop as they screeched or sang out their individual tunes.

The forest began to thin out as I advanced up the trail. Tall grasses and open air gradually replaced the dense trees, roots, and vines. Breaking through the jungle, I found an opening with expansive views of the country below. The lush forest rumbled down the hillside and merged with the cultivated towns and villages, swallowing them up in a sea of green. In the distance was Mount Meru, watching us advance on the slopes of its nearest companion. Meru also wore a skirt of clouds along its midsection, similar to the one I had just escaped on Kilimanjaro.

After a few minutes of peaceful meditation, Lisa, Christian, and Mohamed joined me and we hiked the last thirty minutes of the climb together. We came over a rise to see the first sign of the Machame Camp. A signpost read SLEEPING IN CAVES HAS BEEN PROHIBITED. Just down the trail in a small clearing was the park ranger's hut, a small round metal yurt made of green sheet metal panels on a wooden platform. Nailed to a log next to the hut was another sign. This one read RECEPTION, as if we'd just entered a hotel lobby. The campsite was a series of small clearings in the tall heather and brush. Each clearing was filled with a cluster of tents and hustling porters preparing for dinner. Our tents were just past the reception hut, already erected and with our packs waiting inside.

"Now this is camping," Lisa said, grinning as she climbed into the tent. "I don't have to carry a pack and the tent's set up when we get here, I could get used to this."

"Hello," called a soft voice from outside the tent.

"Hello?" I replied, sticking my head out the tent door.

"Water for washing." It was Juma. He had brought us two steaming pails of hot water. He smiled and set down the water. "Water for washing," he repeated.

"Oh, yeah," Lisa added. "I could definitely get used to this."

Later Juma returned and laid out a small tattered tarp and two stools. He came back, carrying a tray of popcorn, cookies, tea, and cups. "Food," he said, practicing another one of his English words.

"Wow, I'm really getting spoiled," Lisa said. We put on some clean clothes and sat down for afternoon tea. Christian joined us and we sat together sipping our hot brew and grinning in disbelief. Here we were, taking afternoon tea at 10,100 feet above sea level, seated on the side of Mount Kilimanjaro in the East African nation of Tanzania.

We were the captains of the mountain, looking off toward Mount Meru and over the expansive savanna below. It was a good day. It was a great day.

Next to us, Matthias and Suzanne were sitting out front as well.

"Zis is vonderful," Matthias effused, smiling from ear to ear, obviously loving every minute of his time on the mountain.

As evening approached, Juma brought out three bowls and a broth soup for dinner. This was our first course and a holdover from former British colonial rule. Every dinner we'd had in Tanzania started with some form of broth soup. It was nice to see life on the mountain would not be any different. The Tanzanians had more than a hundred years of experience leading Europeans on expeditions; they had it down pat by the time we arrived. But it was also another reminder of the separation between tourists and locals. On Mount Shasta the guides ate and socialized with the climbers. In Tanzania, however, Mohamed spent his time organizing the porters. They ate and slept in a far corner away from us, and there was very little communication between the two groups. I would like to say this reality bothered me. It didn't. I had become strangely accustomed to it already. And besides, Christian's presence now provided what Jeff and Roy had offered Lisa and me earlier in our trip. Throughout the day Christian shared tidbits of the Tanzanian culture, language, and beauty with us.

After dinner we had a final cup of tea. The sun flashed the side of nearby Meru with a red glow, and then it was gone. Within minutes of sunset, the temperature dropped into the forties and we decided to turn in. We wriggled into our warm sleeping bags and immediately drifted off to a comfortable sleep.

I woke shortly before sunrise and could hear people starting to emerge from their tents. The thermometer on my watch said the temperature inside the tent was thirty-four degrees. I rolled over and went back to sleep. Less than an hour later the sun had risen from behind Kilimanjaro and direct light bathed our tent. I could feel the warmth on the nylon walls and the temperature had already climbed to over fifty degrees. It was safe to venture out.

The porters had been up for a while, and it wasn't long before Juma appeared with a pail of hot water. "For washing." He smiled and left us. I splashed some water on my face and rinsed the sleep away. With clear eyes I stood up and took in the bright blue morning. The sun had brushed the clouds away from the entire horizon, and Kilimanjaro, Meru, and the rolling green savanna below were vividly displayed before me. The crisp morning air brought everything into sharp focus. I felt as though I could reach the summit today.

Juma appeared again with our dining tarp and settings. Christian joined us and we sat silently, enjoying the day's peaceful start. Breakfast began with porridge. We each took a few scoops of the runny meal and loaded sugar on top. The steaming substance slid down my throat and warmed my empty stomach. Juma brought over a plate of cold toast for us to share, and three delicately set plates of food for each of us: two eggs, a piece of fruit, and a slightly shriveled hot dog that we all agreed should not be consumed.

After breakfast we stuffed our belongings into our packs and broke down the tent. I strapped it to the back of my pack and set it by a nearby tree. Mohamed returned our water bottles filled with boiled water (to kill any bacteria) and provided us with our trail lunch for the day. Lisa and I left camp shortly before 8:30, the last of the climbers to depart. Even some of our porters were already on the trail ahead of us. But our next campsite was only about six hours away, and we didn't feel the need to rush. We were content to take our time and enjoy the clear morning and open mountain views.

With the rain forest behind us, we were now in the mountain's heather zone, surrounded by tall, dry grass with wispy heath trees standing above. Patches of thistle and dry philippia shrubs dispersed across the mountainside. Damp from the morning dew and riddled with small rocks jutting out of the soil, the trail was steeper and more difficult than yesterday. As I climbed over a small rocky ridge, I looked up and saw the white-topped summit of Kilimanjaro. The white-blue glaciers hung down over the side of the craggy mountaintop. I was amazed at how far we had already come and how close it now looked. This would be easier than I thought.

Christian stopped at this spot as well, eating one of his candy bars and enjoying the view, when Mik arrived with my gigantic pack balanced on his head. The massive load looked as though it had grown even bigger, and he was clearly having some trouble with it.

"*Polenakaze,*" Christian said.

Mik chuckled. "*Assante,*" he said, meaning "thanks," and kept plodding.

"What does that mean?" I asked Christian.

"Something like 'sorry for your troubles' or 'sorry for your work,'" he explained. "If you are walking down the street and you see a friend working in the field, you might say '*polenakaze*' to him. Like, 'Sorry you have to work when I don't.'"

It seemed an appropriate phrase for the situation. Juma came by as we continued waiting. "*Polenakaze,*" I said to him.

He grinned at me. "*Assante.*"

Mohamed joined us next.

"Hey, Mohamed, we're almost there," I said with some cheer, pointing to the glacier-covered summit.

"That's not the summit," he said. "The summit is higher. Behind that."

Deflated at the realization, I put on my daypack and started to trek again. After a few more hours I came out of the high grass to see a large formation of bubbled lava that had hardened centuries ago. At the top of the pile a group of climbers and porters were resting for lunch. I decided to follow their example. I scrambled up and sat down to enjoy my chicken leg and cheese sandwich, when I looked over and noticed Mik sitting next to my pack, taking a well-earned break. He smiled at me, hoisted my pack on his head, and started off. Mik was the first porter I had actually caught up to since we started the climb. I got the impression there was a kind of honor and pride among the porters in being faster and stronger than their wealthy clients. Mik wasn't going to let me beat him up the mountain.

I decided to give him some breathing room while I relaxed. I took out my altimeter watch to gauge our progress. I was the proud owner of a super-duper high-tech, altimeter, compass, multifeatured, official limited-edition Nike Lance Armstrong watch. It could tell me our altitude, rate of ascent, direction, temperature, barometric pressure, time, and date. It had a number of other cool features as well. As soon as I started to play with the buttons, my fellow gearheads swarmed in. The first was a climber from South Carolina, Michael, who was living and working in Geneva, Switzerland.

"What you got there?" he inquired.

"Just trying to figure out what our elevation is," I said.

"Yeah? What reading are you getting?"

I wanted to feel more international and European. So I quickly changed the settings from feet to meters. "About 3,700 meters."

Michael held up his arm to check his own toy. He was packing a wrist computer, as they like to call these. The watch face was a massive round crystal that looked like something from *Star Trek*. "3,834," he said confidently.

Soon another climber had joined us. "What have you got?"

"3,834," Michael repeated.

"That seems a bit low to me," the newcomer responded.

"Really? I have that as a bit high," I chimed in.

"Did you calibrate yours at the last camp?"

"Of course. Did you?"

"Yes, definitely."

"You're measuring based on barometric pressure, aren't you?"

"Yes, but you are too, right?"

We went around and around a few times, trying to fully measure each other's gear choices. In the end we agreed to disagree for the moment and made plans to meet up at the next camp. There we would know the real altitude and could assess the true accuracy of each other's instruments.

When we started to disband, Michael reached into his pack and pulled out a phone. He punched the speed dial and waited for a connection.

"Satellite phone," he said, cupping the mouthpiece. "Have to be able to call people from the summit."

Lisa, Mohamed, and I hiked together in silence for the final hour into Shira Camp. The grade relented and the gentle slope made an enjoyable finish to the day. The forest was completely gone now and our campsite was a massive flat plateau where the Shira volcano had collapsed and had since been absorbed into Kilimanjaro. A few scattered trees below reminded us of the heather zone we had just passed through. But we were now fully in the moorland ecological zone. The tall grass was gone and dry dirt surrounded us with small tufts of grass and squat shrubs that spread out across the landscape.

Climbers from three different routes—the Machame, the Shira, and the Lemosho—converged at Shira Camp. We would all spend the night here and share the trail to the summit. I had heard that more than two hundred tents sprawled across the plateau two weeks ago, but today only a few colored the landscape. I was happy about that. We had plenty of space and it still felt remote. Now that the clouds below had moved in and cut us off from the rest of the world, our campsite felt even more isolated. We were sandwiched between two cloud layers. The one below us, which we had climbed through yesterday, skirted the midsection of the mountain at about 10,000 feet. Above us, another ring was forming on the summit, hiding the glaciers from view. We would climb into that tomorrow.

Once again, Juma greeted us with his wry smile and pails of hot water, followed by the tea and popcorn served on the tattered tarp. After tea I found Matthias, who also had a wrist computer, and asked him what altitude he was reading. According to the map, the camp was at 3,840 meters (12,600 feet). My watch showed 3,850 meters. Matthias was off by almost fifty meters. Lance won. Later, when I ran into Michael again, we compared watches and Lance dominated yet again. I tried not to be cocky.

Despite my climbing success that day, I was developing a headache, so I decided to take a nap. Thirty minutes later I woke to the feeling of a spike being driven into the front of my skull. My head was throbbing and the pain was incredible. The nap had actually made it worse. Rolling over, I realized that the tent had been set up on a slight incline and my head had been on a downhill slant as I slept. For the past half hour blood had been rushing into my skull. Now it was ready to explode.

I was rubbing my temples, struggling to alleviate the pain, when it dawned on my muddled mind that I had drunk only two liters of water and a bit of tea all day. Only two days on the mountain, and I had already forgotten the lessons we had learned on Mount Shasta. I grabbed my one-liter bottle and guzzled the entire contents. Almost immediately, I started to feel better. The spike had been removed from my skull, but the remaining dull pain was a reminder to do better with my hydration in the coming days.

While I was recovering in front of my tent, a Tanzanian man approached with a bag. "You want beer?" he inquired.

The thought of a warm beer at over 12,000 feet made my head spin again and my stomach tighten. Obviously someone wanted to drink up here or else this entrepreneur would not have hauled beer up more than 6,000 feet from the village below. But I couldn't imagine who.

"No, thanks," I replied with a dismissive wave.

"Chocolate?" he tried.

I perked up. Now he had my attention. "What do you have?"

He showed me his supply of candy bars and I bought two with all of the cash I had carried with me. My head felt better almost immediately. I called out to Lisa to see if she wanted any.

"Yes!" came the shout from inside the tent. "I can't eat another chicken leg!"

The cold forced us inside the dining tent for our evening meal. Christian, Lisa, and I sat on the floor with the blue nylon lit by a flickering candle. Tonight's fare, after the soup of course, was a kind of pancake, rice, fried bananas, eggplant, and more chicken. I wolfed it down and again felt the benefits of proper hydration and caloric intake. The bananas in particular were delicious and had probably come from the grove we passed yesterday on our way up. This food was amazing compared with the dry, dehydrated pack meals Lisa and I usually had on our own backpacking trips. Each meal on the mountain, we were learning, featured hot soup, fresh fruit, vegetables, and such carbs as rice, pasta, or potatoes. We had thought that by going with a local outfitter and paying less we would suffer. But so far, it had been luxury.

While we sipped our after-dinner tea, Christian told us he'd heard that three porters had died on the mountain a few weeks ago. They'd been caught in a rainstorm away from camp and the bitterly cold wind had attacked their damp bodies. Hypothermia killed them as they huddled next to some rocks, shivering. The rain and cold had also taken a client's life. All of the victims had been underdressed for the harsh and constantly changing weather. This was a serious reminder to us that we were climbing a mountain. Most of our activity involved hiking and required no special skills or equipment, but this was the highest mountain in Africa—high enough to have snow and glaciers even though it was located only two degrees from the equator. Every year about ten people die on Kilimanjaro, most from altitude sickness, some from hypothermia, and a few from rockfall. The porters bear the largest number of deaths from hypothermia. They wear cotton clothes and carry little extra protection from rain or extreme cold.

Lisa and I crawled into our sleeping bags with these thoughts circling our minds, appreciating the warmth of our retreat all the more. It would be another cold night, with temperatures falling below freezing. The thought of getting out of my bag made me shudder. But after consuming more than four liters of water, it would be impossible for me to avoid venturing into the night at least once to pee. And I had drunk most of my water late in the day.

"I'm staying in my bag tonight," I announced to Lisa as I lay next to her in the dark tent, waiting for sleep. "I'm not getting out to pee!"

"Thanks for sharing," Lisa said before drifting off to sleep.

I had been thoroughly impressed on Mount Shasta that our guide Stephan had been able to accomplish this noble feat for fifteen years. Next to me was an extra one-liter bottle, recycled from a sport drink. Tonight I would relieve myself while still tucked into my cozy sleeping bag, instead of stumbling outside into the freezing night.

I woke at 3:00 AM, unable to ignore my bladder any longer. I fumbled around in the dark and finally found my designated pee bottle. I rolled onto my side, still in my nice warm bag, made the necessary adjustments, and waited anxiously for success. And I waited. Nothing happened. My patience began to wane as my concern began to grow. I had downed almost two liters of water in the afternoon and with dinner. Was my one-liter bottle big enough to meet my current needs?

I was now fully awake and getting frustrated with the process. How the heck did those guys do this on Everest in gale-force winds? I tried getting onto my knees, with the sleeping bag still wrapped around me (and Lisa asleep half a foot away). But all of these frustrated actions were waking me up completely and making me hot. I waited a few more minutes with no results and finally gave up. I threw off the sleeping bag, stumbled into the cold night, and completed my mission without the bottle.

In the morning I woke to the growing light coming through the nylon walls of the tent. But before venturing outside, I forced myself to drink an entire liter of water, just as Stephan had suggested on Shasta. I immediately felt better. The mountain was clear in the morning air and the cool blue sky opened up above us. I could see the individual glaciers now, each one hanging over the edge of the mountaintop. Mohamed informed me that we were looking at the Arrow, Little Breach, and Big Breach glaciers, as well as a sliver of the Heim Glacier.

The other clients packed up their gear and rushed out of camp while Lisa and I dawdled in the clear morning. After sending the porters off, Mohamed walked with us as we ascended the gradual incline toward the glaciers above. The trail, composed of small pebbles and sand, was easy, with a gentle slope as we continued up the plateau. The landscape was strewn with small boulders that had spewed out of the volcano thousands of years ago. Only a few small tufts of grass were hardy enough to survive in the increasingly rugged environment.

When we left Shira Camp, the sun was shining brightly on us, but within an hour the mist began to move in, blocking out the warm sunlight. Cool waves of moisture rolled up the mountain and the temperature fell from sixty to forty degrees. Lisa stopped and put on her shell pants and jacket. The waves had covered us within another hour, and we were completely engulfed in the thick, damp clouds. The temperature was barely above freezing. Now even I was cold. I stopped and put on my shells as well.

Ascending through the fog, we saw three figures ahead of us. After a few minutes, Lisa and I caught up with them. It was two Americans and their guide, each carrying a full pack with no porters assisting them. I was elated that we were actually catching other climbers on the trail. After being dead last for two days in a row, it was our turn to pass others. Our slow-and-steady speed was paying off, and the others would see we had been smart to pace ourselves.

My feeling of superiority didn't last long, however. These three were ascending via the very direct Umbwe Route. This was only their second day on the mountain, and they planned to summit that night. Lisa and I wouldn't summit for two more days. In this sense they were actually three days *ahead* of us. I was demoralized. We were still, in fact, the slowest people on the mountain.

At our lunch break we huddled beside a large rock to stay warm, but it didn't work. We weren't generating enough body heat by sitting still; Lisa started to shiver as she tried to force down some food. We were now at over 14,500 feet of elevation. She had already lost her appetite, and a searing headache was settling in. The cold was too much and we decided to move on. The trail split at this point, with one fork going directly down to our next camp, Barranco, and the other climbing to the famous Lava Tower before descending to camp. We opted for another five hundred feet of elevation gain to see Lava Tower before descending. Despite her obvious discomfort, Lisa wanted to push on. We trudged up the gray trail, able to see only a few feet in front of us.

"Lava Tower," Mohamed announced.

I looked up from the ground and saw mist and clouds. A few feet away I could make out the bottom of what looked to be a large, black volcanic formation. But that was all. It was completely hidden in the fog. We couldn't see more than the bottom few feet while standing right next to it. I snapped a quick picture of Mohamed and Lisa standing in the mist and then we headed on to camp.

The trail started to descend rapidly as we dropped into the Great Barranco Valley. It was a nice change from the morning's uphill grind, and I was encouraged that we'd get into camp early. But Lisa still couldn't go very fast. Her head was pounding and the cold was sapping her energy. The trail was soft and sandy and the pitch was a gradual descent. But her pace hardly changed from the morning's ascent. As we plodded down the mountain, I grew impatient. I just wanted to get to camp. I wanted hot tea and my cozy sleeping bag.

"I want to get to camp, too," Lisa protested, sensing my impatience. Her body just couldn't go any faster; she became frustrated as the altitude sickness took its toll. I offered to carry her pack and tried to get her to eat something. But she was feeling stubborn and insisted on descending under her own power. While the two of us were getting progressively more agitated, Mohamed remained calm and relaxed. He seemed to have no expectations and patiently followed behind, pausing to wait when necessary or slowly shuffling along the trail at whatever pace Lisa and I set.

I thought we were close to camp when we left the Lava Tower but discovered to my dismay that we were still several miles away. We hiked into the fog and clouds for more than two hours without any landmark to define our progress. Finally, by late afternoon, the clouds started to clear below and I caught a glimpse of our destination.

"Hey, I see the camp! You're almost there," I told Lisa. But still, her pace didn't change. Her head hung down and she stared at the gravel trail as she shuffled along one step at a time. I knew Lisa was tough. I'd seen her fight through harder ordeals than a rough hike in cold weather. But it was difficult for me to watch her suffer and not be able to do anything. Like many men, I have a compelling need to fix things for those I care about. So I struggled for some way to help. I suggested to Lisa that I go on ahead to get camp ready so she could have a hot cup of tea and warmer clothes waiting for her as soon as she arrived.

"Go on," she said. "I'm okay. I'll see you at the tent." She was probably more interested in getting rid of me than enjoying a cup of hot tea. But I needed to do *something*. When I told Mohamed I was going on ahead, he recommended against it, suggesting that we stay together.

"Don't worry," I protested. "I can see the camp from here. I'll meet you down there."

And with that I was off, speeding down the trail at a quick trot. I dropped into a minor valley above the camp, and the sides blocked my view of the tents. By the time I had cleared the valley, the clouds had moved in and I could see nothing below. I continued to rush down the mountain, confident there was only one path and that I was headed straight toward camp. After a few more minutes, though, another trail emerged that forked to the left. There was no sign and I had no landmarks below to judge by, but I guessed it was the right way and started down the trail. The farther I went, the more my confidence began to wane. I slowed my pace to a fast walk, then to a slow stroll as I struggled to get my bearings.

The trail dropped into another valley and I was suddenly surrounded by massive giant groundsel trees. They were hauntingly beautiful, looking like a cross between a palm tree and a cactus. Many were as high as twenty feet, and had dead, graying tops that hung above me over the trail. I hadn't seen this valley or these trees from above. I wondered if I was lost and cursed my own stupidity. My ego had caused me to make a rash decision. I had gone ahead of our guide, down a trail I had never been, on a mountain in the middle of East Africa, covered with a thick fog. How stupid could I be? Christian had told us just the previous night about how several people had died from hypothermia because they failed to get into camp after a cold rain.

I began to berate myself and consider my next course of action when the clouds below me started to clear again. I stopped, searching for a sign of camp, straining to find anything in the opening, but it wasn't there. Somehow I had missed it. I was now officially lost.

I paused for a moment, swallowed my pride, and decided to head back up the trail in the hopes of finding Mohamed. Suddenly I heard some rocks fall off to my right. I jerked around to see Mik and one of the assistant guides, Patrice, approaching.

"Hello," Mik said, smiling. "Are you okay?"

"Boy, are you a sight for sore eyes." I doubt he understood the expression, but I didn't care.

"We are worried," he said. "It is late. We look for you. Where is Mohamed?"

"Mohamed and Lisa are coming behind me," I explained, pointing up the mountain.

Mik guided me back to camp while Patrice went back up to find Mohamed. It turns out I had gone off the trail and was headed past the camp, to the east. If I had continued, I would have missed the camp entirely in the fog and gotten lost below. I was very happy to follow Mik back to camp and find Juma waiting with some hot tea.

Lisa, Mohamed, and Patrice joined us in camp another thirty minutes later. Lisa shuffled in with her head low, clearly feeling the effects of the altitude. I got her a cup of tea and helped her settle in before dinner. She was exhausted but satisfied. It turns out that we were the only ones who had gone up to the Lava Tower. Everyone else had decided to head straight to camp. That gave us a small sense of satisfaction.

We all had minor headaches and nausea. Cecelia, the young Canadian woman, thought she was going to vomit, and Lisa suffered from a severe headache. We quietly sipped our tea and everyone turned in shortly after sunset. As I lay in my sleeping bag, I realized that I actually didn't feel too bad, aside from the minor headache. I had been much more careful to drink a lot of water today, and it had paid off.

Shortly before sunrise the next day, I slipped out of my tent and enjoyed a few moments of quiet while everyone else slept. The sun crept over the ridge above and showered my face with warm rays. The sky was clear and the world began to wake around me. I looked up the mountain and had a perfect view of the misty world I had traversed yesterday afternoon. Our camp was perched in the Great Barranco Valley. The Umbwe River, full of cool glacial water, flowed to our east and tall giant groundsel trees sprouted up along the valley sides above. We were surrounded by tufts of small wild flowers and squat bushes. On the far side of the valley a massive lava cliff jutted out of the mountain and rose almost a thousand feet straight up. This was the Barranco Wall and we would have to climb it after breakfast.

Barranco Camp rested at almost the same elevation as Shira Camp. We had climbed more than 2,000 feet in elevation yesterday and descended again. The idea was to "work high, sleep low." By climbing up and returning to sleep at a lower elevation, we hoped our bodies would acclimate to the elevation gain faster. Yesterday's climb had been a gradual ascent. Today we were going straight up the Barranco Wall, right out of camp.

The morning was slower and no one seemed to be in a rush. Our fellow climber Suzanne took the time to hang out some clothes, and Matthias went off to photograph the unique trees on the slopes above. I sipped my tea as the first group of porters departed and began to climb the wall. Each was carrying at least sixty pounds as they grappled up the rock. In many cases they would simply balance the load on their heads and use their hands to scramble up the steeper parts.

Lisa emerged from our tent into the bright morning. She still wasn't feeling well and had a hard time forcing down some breakfast before we left camp. The trail crossed over the Umbwe River right before we started up the Barranco Wall. The fresh meltwater danced over the rocks. It was clear and cool and I couldn't resist it. For three days I had been given water that had been boiled, which to my mind tasted like pennies. I was tired of the acid flavor and salivated at the idea of fresh glacial runoff. I stepped off the trail and hiked upstream to be sure I was away from where it might have been contaminated by people at the campsite. I plunged my hands into the icy water and brought the mountain nectar to my lips. The cool liquid slid down my throat and streamed down the side of my face. I gulped down another handful just to be sure it was as good as I thought.

It was. I quickly dumped out all of my boiled water and filled the bottles with the fresh supply. I should have treated it with my iodine tablets to be sure all bacteria were dead, but I just couldn't bring myself to defile this wonderful gift. I rationalized that there were no camps above that might have spoiled the water, convincing myself that the risk of contamination was low and it was worth it. So I drank it as is. I consumed an entire liter and refilled it right there at the water's edge before hurrying back to the trail to catch up with everyone.

The Barranco Wall was every bit as steep as it had appeared from camp. The trail switched back and forth in lengthy zigzags. At each point where the trail folded back to the other direction, it almost disappeared. We had to scramble up the rocks for several feet to reach the next level. Over and over, I grappled for a good handhold, wedged my feet into any crack I could find, and pulled myself—and my pack full of water—up. I'd traverse another hundred feet or so across the face and repeat this seemingly endless pattern up the thousand-foot face.

At the top the day was still clear and the trail descended gently away. It was easy going now. The others were already ahead, and Lisa, Mohamed, and I followed the rocky route along the mountain with lava boulders strewn around us. It was desolate—only gray rocks and sand in sight. Even the hardy grasses that had been with us for three days were gone, and we hiked across the barren landscape in silence. After another hour the trail rounded a small rise and plunged before us into a deep valley. It dropped over 700 feet to the bottom of a ravine and then rose back up on the other side. As we climbed down into the valley, I kept looking across at the other trail. It was steep, very steep. I wasn't thrilled about the idea of a second climb like that, after the Barranco Wall.

When we reached the bottom, Mohamed veered off the path and marched up the valley to our left and into the lower Karanga Camp. To my relief, I learned that we didn't need to climb the second wall today. Instead, we could relax for the afternoon. Karanga Camp was nestled into a narrow valley under the massive Southern Ice Field. The gravel floor sloped gently down to a small stream running along the side of camp. Up the mountain the Heim Glacier hung over the crater rim and stretched toward us, the white-blue ice radiating in the afternoon sun.

After we settled in, Juma brought us lunch and we sat in the sun eating. Lisa still had a headache and could only force down some fruit.

"That's it. I'm taking the Diamox," she announced. We had both brought a prescription with us just in case. However, we had hoped not to need it. After the rough day into Barranco Camp yesterday, almost everyone had decided to take it. The Canadians, who'd taken their Diamox after last night's dinner, were feeling much better today. Even Christian had started. So Lisa joined the ranks and popped her pills. Only Matthias and I had opted out.

After dosing herself, Lisa lay down for a nap while I hung out some clothes to air out. Christian and Chris headed off for a short hike. Matthias and Suzanne sat outside their tent enjoying hot tea and popcorn. I left them to fill up my water bottles again from the small stream that trickled beside us. I hiked upstream, dreaming about more fresh Kilimanjaro water, when up the trail I noticed one of the porters. He straddled the tiny creek with his pants down and peed right into the water. Although my last batch of the glacial nectar hadn't made me sick, I was playing Russian roulette with my intestines. I was better off taking the boiled water. Who knows how many other porters were peeing in the stream above us?

By the time I got back to camp, Lisa had emerged from her nap with a smile.

"How do you feel?"

"Better," she replied. "Plus, I think the Diamox is starting to work. My whole body tingles." She stood, rubbing her fingers and intrigued with the new sensation. "I hope this is what it's supposed to feel like."

Christian had returned from his hike, to hear Lisa describing the side effect. "Do your fingers and toes tingle too?" he asked.

"Yes, you too?"

"Yeah, I've had it in my fingers and toes all day."

"I feel it all over," Lisa reported. "Maybe I need to take these with more food or just half a pill at a time." I was jealous that I wasn't feeling any drug-induced side effects.

After dinner, Mohamed came by. We engaged in our usual lively conversation.

"Hello. How are you?" he asked.

"Good," we replied.

"Good," he repeated.

"Okay," he continued. "Tomorrow we go to Barafu Camp. Barafu means 'snow' in Swahili. We want to reach Barafu before lunch. So we must leave early. We will have lunch at Barafu and then rest in the afternoon. Tomorrow night we go to the summit. We will leave Barafu at 12:30 in the morning. We want to reach the summit for sunrise."

"Do you think that will be enough time for us?" Lisa asked.

"Hmmm," he thought. "Maybe you will leave a little bit early. Maybe 11:30. Okay?"

"That's fine by us," she said. "Whenever we need to leave to make it to the summit."

"Okay, okay," Mohamed said. "You will leave at 11:30 and Christian will leave at 12:30. No problem."

The next morning we were filled with energy in anticipation of the summit. This was it. I forced down my liter of water and was out of the tent as the first rays of sun came over the valley wall. Lisa was right behind me, and we packed everything up before breakfast. We were determined not to be the last ones out of camp today. Mohamed rushed the cooks and ordered the porters to tear down any tent they could get their hands on. I wolfed down my usual bowl of porridge and an egg sandwich while Lisa nibbled on her cold toast, still with little appetite.

After our hasty breakfast we threw on our packs and jumped onto the trail, the first ones ready to go. It was a triumphant feeling, but it didn't last. Our first task was to climb out of the Karanga Valley up another steep wall. The trail was easier than yesterday, with no rocks to scramble over, but by the time we reached the top, Lisa and I were panting for air. I could feel the effects of less oxygen up here as my lungs heaved. I gulped in the thin air.

After we came out of the valley, the trail leveled off to a moderate incline among small rocks and boulders. The lower cloud layer had already formed around the base of the mountain and Tanzania disappeared. We were alone on the mountain in the sky.

It didn't take long for Christian to catch up and pass us, as he did every day, with a grin and a cheery greeting before zipping on ahead. I had an urge to speed after him, but I forced myself to slow down. *Polepole*, I told myself. Lisa set a leisurely, smooth pace that was perfect. There was no rush. Barafu Camp was fewer than four miles away, and once there, we had nothing to do but wait until 11:30 to summit in the darkness. We took our time as porters rushed passed us.

Mohamed strolled along with us patiently as the trail wandered gently up the rock-strewn mountainside until just below Barafu. There it cut to the left and turned steep as it crept over a rocky outcropping. After a short scramble we were past the hardest part of the day. Ahead of us, it was an almost straight shot up to the rocky campsite.

Barafu Camp was our final resting place before the summit attempt. The campsite sat at 15,100 feet on a desolate rock shelf that jutted away from the Kibo crater section. The platform was barren except for piles of broken rock strewn about everywhere and the Rebmann Glacier peeking at us from the crater rim above. Aside from a small number of tents nestled behind a few rock walls that had been built up as protection from the strong winds, it was a sea of gray chaos. A small green hut perched on the far side; porters were already cooking our afternoon meal.

It was barely noon and the sky was still clear. But the wind was fierce and cut right through my jacket. Once I stopped walking, the cold bit into my skin and forced me into our tent to warm up. Within an hour the clouds began to roll in. It took only a few minutes before the summit section was obscured and we were locked inside the thick mist. The temperature dropped again and I piled on more layers.

It was hard to believe that after only five days we were already well up the mountain. The original explorers of the mountain had taken months to make it this far. The first climbers arrived on the flanks of Kilimanjaro in August of 1861, twelve years after Rebmann had first reported his sighting. They were the German explorer Baron Von der Decken and the English geologist R. Thornton. They attempted to climb the mountain in August but failed even to break through the rain forest. Von der Decken tried again, this time with Dr. Otto Kersten, the following year and they became the first white men to pass the forest zone and into the freezing alpine zone. The same feat took us only one day with well-worn trails, a professional guide, and two porters each. Von der Decken attempted to reach the summit three times in total, failing each time. But the Germans would not be beaten by a pile of rocks. They continued to send able-bodied men up the mountain for another twenty-seven years before finally succeeding.

Tonight was my turn. I lay still, toasty in my sleeping bag, wondering what my fate might be. I nodded off, dreaming of the summit—and the hot shower and beer I would have two days later.

At Barafu Camp before attacking the summit

6

Haraka, Haraka, Haina Baraka

On October 6, 1889, the German geographer Dr. Hans Meyer and the Austrian mountaineer Ludwig Purtscheller were the first to summit Kilimanjaro, reaching the highest point on the African continent. Both Purtscheller and Meyer were adventurers who had yearned to explore and understand the natural world. At the time, Purtscheller was considered the best mountaineer in the Alps, where he was reported to have climbed seventeen hundred peaks. Meyer had graduated from universities in Berlin, Leipzig, and Strasbourg before traveling the world. He had spent months walking through the Philippines. He had visited Cuba, the Middle East, and the United States, and he had spent time in the goldfields of South Africa before making his way to then German-controlled East Africa (the future Tanzania). Meyer wasn't a conqueror or a glory hound— quite the opposite, in fact. He loved nature and respected local people and cultures. He detested the barbaric sport-hunting he saw invading the lands of the local Chagga tribes in Africa, and he lamented the destruction of the wildlife. As he wrote in *Across East African Glaciers*: "The rich preserves of East Africa will share the fate of the vast hunting grounds of South Africa and North America, and in the not far distant future will utterly cease to exist."

Purtscheller and Meyer left the village of Marangu on September 28, 1889. It took them five days to penetrate the rain forest and reach their base camp at about 14,000 feet. They settled in one and a half miles from the foot of the Kibo summit formation and spent the next four days assaulting the mountain to ascend the final 5000 feet. On October 4 they broke past the snowy slopes and reached the crater rim, too exhausted to continue around to the highest point. They tried again on October 6, Purtscheller's fortieth birthday. They left camp at 3:00 AM and spent the next eight hours trudging up the snow, ice, and glaciers until, at midmorning, they stood on the highest point of the Kibo crater rim and planted the German flag. "In virtue of my rights as the first discoverer [I] christened the hitherto unknown and unnamed mountain peak—the loftiest spot in Africa and in the German Empire—Kaiser Wilhelm's Peak," Meyer later wrote in his journal. "Then we gave three cheers more for the Emperor, and shook hands in mutual congratulations."

When the two men reached the summit, only forty-nine Europeans had tried before them. By the time Lisa and I arrived, almost thirty thousand people were attempting this feat every year. A lot had changed. The summit had been renamed Uhuru, meaning "freedom," after Tanzanian independence in 1961. The route to the top was now clear and well traveled. The local guides and porters were conditioned to the cold and altitude, and tourist dollars were a large source of income for them and their families. We were relatively comfortable as we slept (or at least tried to) in our zero-degree down sleeping bags inside a lightweight, reinforced, waterproof nylon tent at the 15,000-foot Barafu Camp.

"Hello," someone said from outside the tent. "Are you awake?" It was Mohamed.

"Yes," I groaned, looking at my watch. It was 10:30 PM. The others wouldn't start for over an hour, but clearly Mohamed was concerned about our slower pace.

"We leave in thirty minutes," he said.

"Okay, we'll be ready."

Lisa was awake now as well. We lay in the darkness for a moment and tried to wake up. Finally, we summoned the courage to emerge into the cold night air, fumbling around in the darkness for our headlamps.

"Did you sleep at all?" Lisa asked.

"A bit. You?"

"A bit. The porters were making a lot of noise out there."

But none of that mattered now. It was summit time. We pulled on multiple layers of thermals, fleece, wool, and shells to protect us from the cold we would experience upon reaching the top. I had agonized for days over exactly what to wear. The harsh wind on the exposed summit would make it feel unbearably cold. But our current position was relatively protected and therefore much warmer. It would be difficult once we started climbing to add any more layers, so we needed to start out wearing what we'd need for the summit. The choice was between comfort now and warmth later.

Lisa squirmed in the confined tent, piling on fabrics of varying degrees of thickness. There is a reason there aren't any famous mountain climbers from Hawaii. Growing up at sea level, wearing a bathing suit and sandals all day, is probably not the best preparation for snow and ice. But here she was, ready to test herself against the harsh summit, even if she was beginning to bear a striking resemblance to the Michelin Man.

For my part, I was a bit more judicious. I knew that I was more comfortable being too cold than too hot. And my legs had never been cold before while hiking, as long as they kept moving. So I opted to forgo a thermal layer for my legs and just went with warm pants and my shell layer. For me, too many layers felt confining. Besides, I grew up in western New York, where winter was measured in feet of snow. Surely I could endure a little cold.

The second issue to contend with was water. It was well below freezing on the summit and the frigid air would quickly ice over any exposed water bottles. So I decided on my CamelBak, strapping it on and then donning my shell jacket over it. I looked like a hunchback, but the water wouldn't freeze if I kept it close to my body. After all, hydration and comfort were more important than looking good.

After almost thirty minutes of squirming around in the small tent, pulling on each subsequent layer, Lisa and I were baking in our clothing cocoons and anxious to get moving. We emerged from our tent and the still night air was a cool compress that dried the sweat on my forehead. It was pitch black on our little rocky outcropping and a relaxing calm had settled over the mountainside. A thin layer of clouds veiled the stars, and all I could see were the scattered boulders illuminated by my headlamp. We could have been anywhere. But we were 15,100 feet up the side of Kilimanjaro. The thought flushed away my drowsiness as we prepared to tackle the last 4,240 feet.

We found Mohamed getting ready in the small hut nearby, accompanied by the assistant guide Patrice. "Patrice will go," Mohamed explained. "If anyone must come back early, Patrice can bring down." Patrice would have been Christian's head guide if he hadn't been folded into our small group. I was comforted by Patrice's presence.

He was an amiable man, a little older than Mohamed. He didn't speak much English but had the air of an unflappable soldier—someone who knew what to do, when to do it, and had done it all before. His calm demeanor was a stark contrast to my growing anxiety, but I was reassured that Lisa and I could split up if necessary because Patrice was coming along.

Lisa and I had discussed what to do if either one of us needed to turn back. In the early days of our training, I had felt we should always stay together. But once I got summit fever, my conviction wavered. On Shasta I had left Lisa waiting behind a rock wall while I bolted the last half mile to the top. Now that we were so close on Kilimanjaro, summit fever was taking me again. I was feeling selfish and wanted to reach the peak, even if I had to go alone. As long as I knew Lisa was safe, I lost all inhibitions about abandoning her and continuing on myself. She understood this and was content for me to go on. I trusted that Patrice would ensure Lisa's safety, and Lisa trusted in Mohamed's competence to bring me back undamaged.

At 11:15 PM we finally left the relative comfort and protection of Barafu Camp and started out in a single line, with Mohamed in front and Patrice in back. The trail was a smooth, sandy path illuminated only by our headlamps. After a few moments the trail jogged left and we began the ascent. At least, I think that is what happened. To tell the truth, I'm not really sure what the trail did. I just followed Mohamed. My headlamp showed only the small patch of gray trail a few feet in front of me. No glorious vistas, no amazing views, no lovely flowers, not even a trail marker—just that small glowing spot of ground that continually rolled out in front of me.

At one point I realized that neither Mohamed nor Patrice had a headlamp or flashlight. Mohamed was, quite literally, leading us up the mountain in the dark. "Mohamed, how many times have you climbed this trail?" I panted as we chugged along.

"Hmmm . . . about a hundred."

"You don't need a light?"

"No," he said, with a chuckle. This was his job, his office. He could find his way up the mountain as easily as I could find my way to the candy machine at work. During the busy seasons—December through February and July through September—Mohamed climbed this route almost every week. He had been doing this for twelve years as a guide, even longer as a porter and assistant guide. While Lisa and I huffed and puffed behind him, Mohamed strolled along the invisible trail just as he had last week and the weeks and years before that.

I would love to report that the excitement of alpinism and the adventure of mountaineering culminated in an apex for our final summit bid. I would like to wax eloquent about the immense difficulty we surmounted and the incredible impediments put in our path by the mountain. But I was slowly realizing a little secret the mountaineer-writer Jon Krakauer never mentions: mountain climbing is actually pretty boring. At its core it's just hours and days of walking uphill. Of course, there are exciting moments and beautiful vistas, but those are just drops in the placid lake of mind-numbing slogging over dirt and snow.

After the first hour, following Mohamed up the final trail, I was already bored by the tedium of it all. Watching grass grow would have been more thrilling. Without any distractions, my mind wandered to anything concrete it could find and finally settled on analyzing my own body. I listened to my labored breath, felt the dry air inside my throat, observed my lungs struggling to pull in the much-needed oxygen, and watched my legs slumping along over the dirt. I was getting completely lost in my own physical experience when Lisa interrupted.

"I think I'm going to go back," she said, panting. I was startled out of my reverie.

"What?" I stopped and turned toward her.

"I think I should turn back," she said again between breaths. "I don't think I'm going to be able to make it to the summit (*pant pant*). If I'm not going to make it, then (*pant pant*), I'd rather save my energy for the fourteen-mile hike to the next camp (*pant pant*) this afternoon."

Her mind was working faster than mine was. For more than an hour she had been thinking about how hard this summit climb was—and how much harder the day ahead was going to be. We had four miles and 4,000 feet of climbing to reach the summit before turning around and hiking another fourteen miles back down and to the next camp. Lisa had decided it was better to save her energy and enjoy the hike down than to be exhausted and miserable and perhaps fail to reach the summit anyway.

Mohamed turned around and looked at her for a moment. "Okay," he said plainly, and walked back to Patrice. He never said another word to Lisa, never tried to convince her to continue. Later Lisa told me she thought Mohamed had never believed she'd make it.

"Are you sure?" I asked.

"Yeah," she said. "For me, it's more about the climb than the summit. I'm okay. Don't worry. You go on," she said, encouraging me with a weak smile. As we spoke, Mohamed gave Patrice instructions for taking Lisa back to camp. I don't speak Swahili, but I know I heard *polepole* (slowly) repeatedly. Patrice nodded his understanding, and after a few minutes Mohamed let them go.

"Okay," Mohamed said. *"Polepole,"* he told Lisa one last time.

"Good luck," Lisa said, turning back to me. And then they descended.

As Lisa started down the hill, I looked at my altimeter watch. She had made it to almost 16,000 feet, higher than either of us had ever been before. That was a worthy accomplishment.

Seeing them depart, Mohamed turned back up the mountain.

I was disappointed that Lisa wouldn't join me on the summit, but I also understood. She didn't have summit fever. For days we had enjoyed sweeping vistas of the Tanzanian savanna, wildflowers, and rock formations. We'd had stimulating conversation with people from all over the world. But for the past hour, all we had was rolling gray ground and the sound of our own labored breathing. This wasn't fun. This was work. Now I understood what I had read somewhere, years ago: "Enjoy your suffering. That's what alpinism is all about."

Mohamed and I continued up the mountain. I looked below and tried to make out the descending forms of Lisa and Patrice, but they were long gone. Far below, I saw a herd of tiny lights coming toward us. It was after midnight and other climbers were starting their ascent. We plodded our way up the dirt slope for another hour or so, stepping over stones here and there. The trail was an endless series of switchbacks, back and forth, back and forth, to make the steep ascent a more manageable grade.

As time creaked on, the lights spread out over the mountain. The batteries in my headlamp died from the cold and I quickly exchanged them for the warm ones I had stashed in my pocket. Some of the lights were getting closer. After a while, two Swiss women caught us and quickly passed. They strolled by me, hands in their pockets, looking as if they were walking through a park while I could hardly catch my breath. I chucked my trekking poles into the soft dirt. I hated these women immediately. How could this be so hard for me and so easy for them? Living in the Alps had probably provided a slight advantage. I tried to let it go.

Eventually Christian and his guide, Ally, caught up with me. They had left thirty minutes after Lisa and me but had made good time. We trekked together for a while, not speaking, just panting along. Oxygen was a much more precious commodity than conversation. Soon Christian and Ally pulled ahead of us. I trudged along, annoyed with their passing me. In frustration, I decided that Lisa's slower pace for the first hour was responsible. Not a very nice thought, but I was desperate for any excuse.

It was shortly past 3:00 AM and we were at almost 17,000 feet. For hours I had been waiting for the moon to rise, hoping it would shed enough light to reveal something, anything, that would make the climb more interesting. Finally, a sliver of moon appeared on the horizon . . . and made no difference whatsoever. The thin form cast almost no light and the darkness continued to envelop us. I was heartbroken.

My mind wandered farther up the hill and into the future, looking for anything to grab onto. The sun would not rise for another three hours; that seemed like an eternity. The idea of this continued boredom, with constant reminders of my own suffering and no possible distraction, was completely disheartening. To make matters worse, Suzanne and Matthias passed me as well. Suzanne was suffering but looked strong. Matthias cruised by with a smile and an encouraging "You can do it!" Did I mention he lives in the Alps, too?

And then we were alone again, just Mohamed and me on the side of a 19,340-foot mound of volcanic rock and dirt in East Africa. We trudged along in silence except for my panting and the chuck of my trekking poles digging into the dirt.

Pant. Chuck. Step. *Pant. Chuck.* Step. *Pant. Chuck.* Step.

I was constantly thirsty now and kept taking small sips of water. I sipped so often that I began to worry about running out of water. I tried to pace myself between sips to ensure I'd have enough. As we continued our gradual march, I began to lose control of my thoughts. My mind seemed to float above me, like an impartial observer watching a movie. My aching legs and my winded breathing became part of the movie. Even time shifted to a swelling and flowing eddy, no longer linear in its progression.

I looked at my watch and saw that it was 4:15 AM. Lisa had left us hours ago and was probably safely asleep by now. A fog crept in from the corners of my brain as I tried to focus. My head ached, I felt dizzy, and nausea was growing in my throat and stomach.

Am I alright? a voice wondered in my brain.

My eyes wandered over the ground in front of me, trying to find something to focus on in the darkness. This brought the dizziness to the front of my skull with a vengeance. Slowly my knees unhinged and I slumped onto the fine gravel. I found myself on my knees, held upright by my trekking poles. It felt good to rest for a moment, to not be moving. I thought about staying there, but something in my brain shouted that this was bad.

I sagged forward for a moment, took a few deep breaths, then pulled myself up. I stepped forward with more control than before and began again. I concentrated on my breathing and tried to draw the thin air deep into my lungs. I focused my entire consciousness on my body and forced it to respond as I commanded. It was working.

After what seemed like another hour or two, I looked back down at my watch. It was 4:19 AM. I checked again but still it was 4:19. Had I read it wrong before? Perhaps it had been 3:15 earlier? Yes, that was it. I focused again and memorized the time. 4:19 AM. Now I was sure it was correct. I put the watch in my pocket and lumbered on.

With each step my body felt heavier. My legs ached with lactic acid building up in my muscles. My hands were getting weak from clutching my trekking poles. I wrapped the straps tight around my wrists to secure my grip. I took too many sips of water and tried to fight off the oppressive thirst. After what seemed like another hour, I looked at my watch again. 4:22 AM! My mind searched for some possible explanation for this strange phenomenon. Clearly hours had passed and yet my watch did not register this fact. I couldn't rectify my perceptions with reality.

Pant. Chuck. Step. *Pant. Chuck.* Step. *Pant. Chuck.* Step.

I stumbled on in darkness with Mohamed wandering along in front of me. The dizziness rolled to the front of my head again. My knees buckled and I went down like a sack. I held myself upright with my trekking poles for a moment before slowly sinking all the way to the ground. Mohamed came back and helped me up.

"I'm fine, I'm fine," I slurred in protest. My mouth felt detached from my head and I couldn't articulate the words properly. "Let me just take a break," I sputtered as Mohamed helped me to sit on a nearby rock. It seemed as though only a moment had passed before Mohamed was pushing me to my feet.

"Don't stop too long," he warned. "You get too cold."

And we started again. I took a long breath and pulled the precious air deep into me. The fog cleared.

"Focus!" I shouted inside my head. "Breathe!" I kept reminding myself. "Breathe!" And it worked. Again I regained control over my body. We moved with deliberation and, dare I say, some speed.

After another hundred yards, though, it all began to slip away again. The experience was like trying to hold onto water. No matter how hard I tried, I felt control of my limbs and thoughts gently slide away. My pace slowed to a crawl as my legs sagged and shook. Again, my body slumped to the ground.

As I lay there, my mind began to register a new sensation. From a distance I began to feel cold. I felt as though I was standing in icy water on a hot day, and it was almost refreshing and energizing. The feeling was concrete and my mind fixed on it. As the cold sensation slithered up my legs, I realized they were shaking.

Mohamed noticed this new phenomenon and immediately bent over and started to rub my legs. I heard him softly say, "Your legs are shaking. Not good." I didn't understand what it meant. "You must keep moving. You must keep warm," he ordered.

I breathed deeply and stood, clutching my trekking poles. After another deep breath, I continued, walking with newfound focus and determination.

One hundred yards later, my focus evaporated and I fell again. This time Mohamed didn't even wait. He grabbed my arm and hefted me to my feet. He marched on, propping up my weight and propelling me up the summit.

"I'm okay," I slurred in protest and pulled myself away from him. I kept walking on my own for another fifty yards before flopping again to the earth. Mohamed supported me again and we kept walking.

"Does it get better?" I asked weakly. "If I keep going, will I get better?"

"Okay," Mohamed assured me.

I was worried about altitude sickness, or acute mountain sickness (AMS). I was operating on almost half the normal amount of oxygen I was accustomed to. If my body hadn't adjusted to the lack of oxygen, the results could be dangerous. AMS doesn't catch everyone, and there's no telling who it will affect and how. It just depends on how susceptible one's physiology is to altitude.

The symptoms are typically things like headaches (check), fatigue (check), shortness of breath (check), nausea (check), unsteadiness and dizziness (check), and more. The more severe forms of mountain sickness are high-altitude pulmonary edema (HAPE) and high-altitude cerebral edema (HACE). HAPE is the collection of fluids in the lungs and can result in labored breathing, coughing blood, anxiety, and pale skin. HACE is even worse. The brain swells and brings on headaches, hallucinations, and even death. Both HACE and HAPE can be fatal if not treated in time. The idea of a distracting hallucination was appealing, but death didn't seem like a good time.

"I can do it," I sputtered, pulling away from Mohamed again. He seemed almost pleased every time I did this. Perhaps he was testing me. I didn't really care. But I wasn't going to be carried up the mountain. It was better to fail then to succeed as a fraud.

I continued for another fifty yards under my own power. My body swayed with each step. I gave up trying to control my breath and panted helplessly. Finally, I lost control again for the last time. My body crumbled completely and I disintegrated to the ground. I felt my entire body fall to pieces from within. Tears streamed uncontrollably from my eyes as my arms and legs flopped onto the cold gravel.

My trekking poles sunk beside me, useless. My body had revolted and every last vestige of control I had was gone.

I lay on the sandy earth and looked up at the sky feeling completely helpless. The clouds had cleared and the stars shone bright in the early morning sky. My limbs were cast about me and all I could do was look at the heavens. I felt a strange calm float over me. My limbs became numb and an eerie feeling of safety and warmth washed over my whole body.

The stars were beautiful. I don't think I'll ever forget them. It was as if I were looking at them for the first time. All desire seeped from me. I didn't care about the summit any more. I didn't care about anything. I felt an overpowering sense of peace just lying still, not moving a single muscle. I had a lovely tingling sensation all over, and I liked it. Clearly this was an improvement.

If Mohamed said anything to me, I didn't hear it. My thoughts strayed up to the stars before coming back to earth. Then I began to think about Lisa, asleep 3,000 feet below me. A shred of consciousness poked in and made me nervous. When people suffer from hypothermia, they are eventually overcome by a feeling of warmth, sometimes to the point of feeling overheated. Many hypothermia victims are found almost naked, having taken off all their clothes.

I began to hear a mantra in the back of my mind: *Nobody is dying on this mountain tonight.* It repeated itself again and again.

Nobody is dying on this mountain tonight. Nobody is dying on this mountain tonight.

My mind was slowly fighting its way back to reality when I heard a group approaching from below. It was one thing to die on the mountain, quite another to do it while everyone else effortlessly marched by.

"Everything okay here?" It was John, the Canadian father, and his son and daughter.

"That you, John?" I slurred as I tried to pull myself together in front of guests. I managed to look up and caught a glimpse of John before my vision went blurry again. He looked terrible. Then I realized that although he looked bad, he was still standing. He was twice my age and still going. Here I was falling apart all over the mountain. I was overcome by shame and vanity. I wondered how bad I must look lying sprawled on the ground, a complete wreck.

"How you doing, John?" I asked, trying to sound more upbeat than I felt.

"It's tough," he allowed. "How about you?"

I hesitated. "I'm thinking about heading down." I didn't know I had been thinking this, and yet out it came. I was thinking about quitting.

"You do what you have to do," John replied in a weary but encouraging voice. "You've done a good job."

While John and I spoke, their guide, Felix, fished out a Thermos and handed me a cup of lukewarm tea. "Here, drink this," he said, thrusting the cup into my hand.

I slurped up the sweet tea while Felix and Mohamed exchanged a few words in Swahili. Felix took the cup back, put his Thermos away, and announced that his group needed to continue. John hesitated. For a moment I thought he might decide to go back down too. But he didn't. He opted to fight on, and I was impressed—and more than a little jealous.

"Good luck," he offered, and then continued up the hill while I lay there.

"We are only a hundred meters below Stella Point," Mohamed encouraged. "If you make it to Stella Point, I can give you a certificate. Only thirty minutes."

The idea of a certificate seemed ludicrous at this point. I ached for the summit but wasn't sure how far I could push my body. Would my own competitiveness and vanity drive me to hurt myself? Was I endangering myself or merely lacking the mental strength to push myself to my actual limit?

As I lay there on the frozen ground, a cold logic took over and I made my choice: "We go back." I tried to stand up and seem determined but ended up only lumbering over onto my side. "We go down," I said again, trying to convince myself as well.

"One hundred meters. Only thirty minutes. I can help you," Mohamed said, giving me every option he could. "You are very close."

"No," I said, panting. "We go down."

"Very close," he said again. "Are you sure? I can help you."

I was tempted. One hundred meters in elevation gain was a little over a quarter mile in distance. But the idea of spending the next thirty minutes falling to the ground and being dragged by Mohamed wasn't appealing. I didn't see the point in being carried up the mountain. It would feel like a lie, and I would be ashamed to be a part of it.

"No," I said definitively. "We go down." I stood up on my wobbly legs and began to walk downhill. I didn't know where I was going, I just wanted to move. I had made my decision and it was time to go.

Mohamed moved quickly to grab my arm, to stabilize me as I almost fell. We didn't say another word. We started down the soft sand and gravel, descending rapidly. On our ascent we had zigzagged back and forth to reduce the grade. On the descent, however, we took the slope straight on. Each time I stepped forward, my foot slid for a yard down the snowlike sand. We were skiing, and the speed was exhilarating, if a bit worrying.

My legs were not suddenly stronger with my decision to descend. I still had several miles to go and no real strength. All I wanted to do, with every fiber of my body, was lie down. I just wanted to stop. But I knew I couldn't. For a while Mohamed continued to support me by hooking my elbow with his powerful arm. I became frustrated by this. I was ashamed to have to turn back while so many others had been able to continue. I pulled away from Mohamed and tried to descend on my own. If I would fail, at least I would fail under my own power.

Getting back to camp seemed to take an eternity. After a while the sun began to rise, but I didn't stop to watch it. The gray sandy hill slowly transformed into a soft reddish brown under my feet. The light was refreshing and the morning rays heated my face. The camp was nowhere in sight—I had a long way to go. I plodded on, trying to ignore my body with each aching, wobbling step.

It had taken us over five hours to trudge up toward the summit. It took only about two to return. I stumbled into camp around 7:30 AM, absolutely exhausted. Mohamed guided me to my tent. Lisa came out, startled to see me.

"Are you okay?" she asked, with great concern in her eyes. I knew I must have looked terrible.

"I'm fine," I mumbled and fell to the ground. I stripped off my boots, crawled into the tent, and flopped onto my sleeping bag. As soon as I stopped moving, my body began to shake uncontrollably. The cold seeped through my bones and I felt a freezing shudder emanate from within me. I tried to calm myself and stop shaking, but I couldn't control it. And after a moment I didn't have the strength enough to care. I lay there and let my body convulse.

Lisa threw her sleeping bag on top of me, along with any coats and clothes she could find. She rubbed my shivering body through the nylon layers and I drifted off. For the next two hours I slipped in and out of consciousness, shivering and huddling under the warm pile of nylon and down. Slowly the shaking subsided, the warmth crept back into my bones, and I began to recover.

Our guide, Mohamed

Eventually I warmed up enough to emerge from the toasty tent in search of food. Juma gave me a hot bowl of porridge, which I ate in a sulk. I was feeling better now and my increased energy went straight to being angry with myself. Lisa wisely gave me space as I tried to come back to reality. Mohamed approached me.

"How are you?" he asked.

"Fine, thanks."

"Okay, we leave in twenty minutes for Rau Camp," he said, and then walked away.

Lisa packed up the tent. I sat in the door of the hut and watched Christian return from his summit. He was exhausted but jubilant. The Swiss women who had passed me on my way up had been in camp for hours and were already leaving for Rau Camp. They had reached the summit thirty minutes before sunrise and decided it was too cold to wait for the view. As the Tanzanians say, there is no blessing for being first.

I pulled on my daypack and Lisa, Mohamed, and I silently marched out of camp to our next destination. The hike down from Barafu was lovely, really. We descended the far side of the lava formation we had climbed the previous day. For the first few hours we hiked in silence across the gentle alpine desert trail with the peak behind us and the mountain sloping away before us. Plants and short grass began to appear; eventually we saw bushes and finally heather. I didn't take the time to enjoy the scenery. I was still tired and just wanted to rest. But I could also feel myself getting stronger with every step down the mountain. Each foot lower brought more and more oxygen, and I could feel it all around me. The air grew thicker and even 12,000 feet felt like sea level.

Christian, Suzanne, and Matthias caught up with us, and by late afternoon we made our way into Rau Camp at 10,100 feet. Typically climbers descend to Mweka Camp, but it was closed for some construction so we used Rau instead. Once again, our tent had passed us on the trail, thanks to the trusty porters, and was set up, waiting for us. We took off our boots and slid inside the tent to lie down. I lay silent next to Lisa, finally able to stop moving and relax. It felt wonderful. But as my strength continued to return, doubts emerged. If I was recovering this quickly, then surely I could have gone farther up the mountain.

It started to sprinkle softly and the light drizzle coated the tent, allowing us an excuse to stay inside. Mohamed came to the tent door.

"Everyone okay?" he asked.

"We're fine," Lisa replied.

"How many people don't make the summit, Mohamed?" I asked.

"Okay," he said. "It happens. It happens a lot." Mohamed had seemed distant during the descent, but I wondered if I was just projecting my disappointment onto him. He left us to checked in on the others.

"Are you okay?" Lisa asked gently.

"Yeah. I'm fine."

"Are you going to be okay with this?"

"I don't know." I really didn't know. I had no idea how my failure was going to affect me.

"How disappointed are you?"

"Moderately."

"Just so I can prepare," she asked, "do you think this is going to be a big obsession for you, or just a minor annoyance?"

I laughed. She knew me well. I'd obsess over this for a while. That wasn't the question. The question was just how much and for how long. "I don't know," I said, smiling.

"Well, don't worry. You impressed me." Lisa said, grinning. "I'll still marry you."

The trail down from the Machame Route

7

Out of Africa

The night was peaceful as we slept on the grassy field of Rau Camp. I woke just before sunrise, well rested and alert—and acutely aware of a horrible odor emanating from my sleeping bag. My head was tucked inside my warm down bag, and every time I inhaled, my nasal passages were filled with the decidedly unpleasant stench of seven days of sweat and grime. I really needed a shower.

Lisa squirmed next to me. "Wow, I really need a shower," she mumbled, half asleep.

I stuck my head outside my bag to escape my own aroma and to breathe the fresh air. "Um . . . yeah, you do," I replied. "But so do I." Seven days without a shower. There was no hiding it: we stunk.

It was early and still cold outside the tent. But it had to be better than inside. I pulled on the cleanest clothes I could find and stepped into the crisp morning. The campsite was quiet as others slumbered in the tents strewn across the grassy field bordered by thick bushes. The sun was rising and casting a warm, red glare onto the Mawenzi peak off to the east. Hans Meyer, the German geographer, had climbed that peak a few days after his summit success. I was done climbing.

I took out a few cleaning wipes and scoured as much of my body as possible, but it made little difference. As I struggled, Matthias emerged from his tent nearby and I quickly stopped my scrubbing. Here was a seasoned alpinist. He had been on the side of mountains for weeks on end. And here I was worried about not having a shower after only seven days. I felt like a wimp.

"Ohhh!" he grunted, stretching. "I can't vait for a hot shower. I love zee mountains, but enough is enough. I need a shower!"

We joined Christian for our final meal on the mountain. My energy returned with breakfast. The sleep and oxygen had restored my strength. My failed summit experience was almost a full day behind me now and some of the frustration had faded. But I was plagued by doubt and embarrassment. How would I explain this when I got home?

"I don't know if I should tell you this, Dan," Christian started.

"Go ahead."

"When we passed you on the mountain, Ally said he didn't think you were going to make it. I was surprised to hear him say that since you looked pretty strong to me. But I guess he saw something."

I wasn't encouraged. Ally knew just by the look of me that I wouldn't make it. He knew I would give up. The idea of him seeing my failure made things worse.

"I almost didn't make it myself," Christian offered. "When we got to Stella Point, I was exhausted and felt terrible. I thought about going down. Then . . . I don't know. It was a bit strange really."

"What?"

"Well, Ally put his hand on my back to support me. And you know what? It worked."

"Really?"

"Yeah, I don't know why, but just him putting his hand on my back reassured me a bit and gave me enough energy to continue."

After breakfast we packed up and prepared to hike out. The signpost at the edge of the campsite stated that the hike out should take between five and seven hours. I felt the sting of my failure, so close to the summit, and decided I needed to prove myself. I needed to beat *something*. I told myself I was going to get to the gate in fewer than seven hours, damn it.

The porters piled their loads onto their heads and shot out of camp. They were anxious to be done and get home. I had heard it was a point of honor for them to beat all the clients off the mountain the last day. Christian decided he was going to test that theory and ran off to quickly grab his things and give chase.

Lisa and I dashed out of camp before the others. We started off with a strong pace and looked destined to beat the time. But once we entered the rain forest, the sky disappeared behind the thick canopy and the trail returned to the slick, muddy substance we had seen seven days earlier. Several trees had fallen over the path and large roots were exposed, making it difficult to hike. As the morning passed and the trail became more challenging, Lisa's pace slowed. Christian had rushed past us to catch the fleeing porters, and Matthias and Suzanne soon trucked past us as well.

"Seven hours. No problem." I tried to encourage Lisa.

"I'm not in any rush," she explained. "But you can go ahead if you want to." That was all I needed to hear. I was off. Lisa enjoyed her last few hours on the mountain, taking it all in at a leisurely pace while I doubled my speed and almost jogged down the muddy path as it slithered through the forest. After less than an hour, I passed Matthias and Suzanne. The trail got wider for a few miles and turned into a dirt road.

Another mile later I came around a long bend and was surprised to find most of the porters sitting by the side of the trail, lounging in the short grass. Their heads shot up at the sight of me, surprised to see a *mzunga* so close behind. A few of them threw on their packs and jumped onto the trail in front of me, bolting down the hill to stay ahead. This was more than enough encouragement. I trotted down the road trying to catch the porters while trying not to look like I was trying to catch them. But before I could reach them, the trail passed under the concrete Rau Gate. I looked down at my watch.

It had taken me seven hours and seven minutes. I had just missed my goal.

Christian sat in the grass by the side of the trail, having just arrived himself. There were a few small wooden shacks in the tree-covered meadow—vendors selling t-shirts and snacks. I joined Christian and we sat against a tree, sipping orange sodas and waiting for the others to arrive. One by one they showed up. Our well-worn packs were loaded onto a nearby bus, and we headed back to the hotel for much needed hot showers.

We, the triumphant band of climbers, sat together over dinner, joking and chatting about our adventure. Everyone seemed to be back to normal with the return to oxygen and civilization, except for John. He looked like he'd aged ten years. He was exhausted from the summit and sat hunched over his plate. But he had made it, even if it had cost him dearly. Everyone had made it to the summit, except for Lisa and me. This thought would gnaw at me for some time to come. The next morning the group dispersed. Matthias and Suzanne went on safari while the Canadians traveled to Zanzibar. Christian planned to stay a few more days in Moshi for work. Lisa and I made our final souvenir purchases before taking the shuttle back to Nairobi. The following day, we flew home.

Back in San Jose, we tried to adjust to the modern world, but everything felt so strange after Africa. Clothes, food, restaurants, and all the conveniences we once took for granted seemed opulent, even wasteful. Every time I brushed my teeth, I was amazed that I could drink water right out of the tap. Something as simple as ready access to clean, safe water seemed luxurious.

I returned to work and found it odd that everything was the same as when I had left. Lisa and I had spent more than two weeks in a world we could have only dreamed of before. We had returned different people. We had changed, but life in California hadn't changed a bit. My coworkers and friends wanted to hear all about Kilimanjaro and our adventures. But I was reluctant to share. I wanted to tell them all about Tanzania and everything we had seen, but not my failure on the summit.

"How was Tanzania?" everyone asked, always their first question. I relished each opportunity to share that magical place with people.

"Did you make it to the top?" was always the second question. I had dreaded that question even before returning to the States. But after trying to answer it ten different times, I discovered that my explanations didn't matter. The conversation was always the same.

"Did you make it?"

"No."

"Why not?"

"I got hypothermia and altitude sickness."

"Oh . . . so . . . how far did you get?"

"Almost 18,000 feet."

"Oh . . . that's good. . . . Well, welcome back."

I couldn't decide which was more frustrating—the fact that I failed or the fact that it really didn't make any difference to anyone but me. And then there was the leprechaun—my elfish, portly coworker who'd actually climbed Kilimanjaro. After avoiding him for as long as possible, I ran into him in front of the coffee machine. My teeth clenched as I repeated my failure to him.

"Don't worry. I completely understand," he offered. "In our group of ten, I was the only one to make it. But we took the Marangu Route." He had successfully summited via the route that has the lowest success rate; I had failed on the route with one of the highest. Although I appreciated his kind words, they twisted a knife in me and made my shame even more acute.

Not all of my discussions about Kilimanjaro were so painful, though. I spoke with a medical student who was planning to do the climb. After hearing my story about the boy and his blind grandfather on the bus, she solicited antibacterial eye drops from her hospital and took an entire case with her to Moshi. I gave a presentation to the Rotary Club about the climb and Tanzania. One of the attendees informed me that he ran his church's thrift shop.

He escorted me to the store and gave me three large plastic bags full of warm clothing to ship to the Kilimanjaro Porters Assistance Project.

I enjoyed sharing my experience with people and slowly learned to accept my failure. I realized that the positive aspects of our trip vastly outweighed my disappointment on the summit. I volunteered to speak at a local Sierra Club meeting about it. I spent hours poring over my pictures and creating a detailed presentation with information about Tanzania, our itinerary, packing, training, and anything else I could think of. I crammed the talk with as much African beauty and information as I could. One evening after work, I headed over to the local outdoor store where the monthly meetings took place. Lisa joined me, sitting in the back, ready to provide any finer details people might request. I launched into my pictures and waxed eloquent on the beauty of Tanzania, the challenges of the mountain, and the glory to be had for the few who tackled it. When I came to the end of my presentation, a gentleman in the back raised his hand.

"What was it like on the summit?"

I had hoped to gloss over the summit portion. To conceal my failure, I had "borrowed" another picture of climbers at the top and included it in my presentation. To be fair, I never said it was me on the summit, but it would have been possible for someone to walk away with that impression. I looked to the back of the room and saw Lisa offering a supportive smile.

"I never made it to the summit," I replied.

"Why not?"

"I got hypothermia and altitude sickness."

"Oh . . . so . . . how far did you get?"

"Almost 18,000 feet."

That was the end of it. But these people weren't your

everyday Joe Public or even weekend warriors. These were experienced mountaineers who loved nothing better than to make their lungs heave while stomping to the top of any rocky peak they could find. They understood the dangers that climbing mountains present, and that people need to turn back from time to time. Many had even been forced to turn back themselves by bad weather, lack of time, or injury. I could only hope that this group understood why I had turned back.

However, my life wasn't all angst and anguish. In fact, it was quite the opposite. Although my "failure" at Kilimanjaro weighed heavily on me, I found myself somewhat lighter and more easygoing after Tanzania. The culture and people had gotten into my blood. I found myself less upset about problems at work, more willing to laugh and to connect with strangers. Before leaving for East Africa, I had carried much of my New York cynicism with me, but Tanzania purged me of it. No matter how bad things got, I still had vivid memories from one of the most beautiful places on the planet. Nothing could erase that or the lessons I'd learned from my friendly hosts.

Other things going on in my life helped me smile more as well: Lisa and I spent the winter months planning our wedding. After almost three weeks of being together nonstop in Africa, we knew we were compatible. We'd survived traveling together, failure on the mountain, and an obscene amount of BO. It was a great start to any relationship.

We flew to Hawaii for the event, and on March 9 we stood on the beach along the North Shore of Oahu and pledged our love in front of friends and family. We danced for the first time as husband and wife while the sun set beyond the ocean, showering the island with its final rays. We could hear the soft sound of the surf against the shore as Etta James sang "At Last." The moon rose and cast its pale light over the beach. We dined on khalua pig, poi, chicken, long rice, and other Hawaiian favorites. My entire family, much to my amazement, had flown in from across the country to be a part of it all. I was deeply touched that they'd come so far, for us.

As the party raged and our wives took over the dance floor, my three brothers and I enjoyed a beer together.

"Think you'll ever go back to Kilimanjaro?" my younger brother asked.

"I don't know, Matt. . . . I'd like to. . . . Hard to say though," I said, kind of stumbling over the thought.

Then he really surprised me. "I'd like to climb it someday. Maybe if you go back, I'll come with you. You know, not now, but later." And then we drank more beer. I didn't take him seriously.

Lisa and I spent more than three weeks in Hawaii. By the time we got back to San Jose, it seemed different to us. All we could see were strip malls, freeways, and concrete. After more than two weeks in the natural beauty of Africa and three in Hawaii, we just couldn't take the urban sprawl anymore. We decided we needed to move to some place more picturesque. As we explored the nearby mountains, we became enchanted by the Lake Tahoe area—the crystal clear lake, the snow-capped mountains, and the remote feeling in the small towns. Lake Tahoe itself is one of the largest lakes within the United States. It's the third deepest lake in North America, and one of the most beautiful places we'd ever seen. So we rented a little house in the mountains, just over the Nevada state line, along the lake's north shore.

On a single Saturday afternoon we packed up our tiny studio apartment in San Jose and navigated our rental van up the foothills into the Sierra Nevada to our new home. We had been living at sea level and had packed up the truck without incident. But our new home sat at more than 7,000 feet above sea level; the difference in altitude was immediately apparent. The house had two flights of stairs from the street to the kitchen. By the time I got a box from the truck to the top floor, my chest was heaving and my head swimming. After only a few heavy boxes, my legs ached. By the time we were done unloading the truck, we were panting, exhausted, and hurting all over.

But what our new home lacked in oxygen, it more than made up for in everything else. The house was tucked into a small community in the mountains, two miles away and a thousand feet of elevation above the nearby town. From our front deck we had a fantastic view of the surrounding mountains. The scene was filled with white fir, Jeffrey pines, and the occasional quaking aspen trees. It was a short hike to the Tahoe Rim Trail that circled the entire lake. That was our backyard. Our frontyard was Lake Tahoe itself. The azure lake was filled with clear waters and ringed by majestic peaks. This was the perfect place for us to live and train.

I'd had it in my mind for a while that I wanted to return to Kilimanjaro. I loved the idea of living at over 7,000 feet of elevation and hoped that living and training at this altitude would make it possible for me to reach the summit next time. With ready access to so many mountains, it would be a lot easier to get in shape. My first real physical test came not from hiking but from cycling. After living in Tahoe for a few weeks, I decided it was time for me to start bicycling again. I sped down the steep, two-mile hill in front of our house and took a leisurely jaunt along the lakeside. The views were breathtaking; each scene of the magical lake inspired me to go farther. After more than an hour of sightseeing, I turned around and made my way back to the foot of the mountain where our house stood.

Now it was time for work. I dropped my gear and dug in for the long push up. The first mile of the climb looped upward through a small housing development and into the trees. I was breathing hard and sweating, but I was progressing. Then the road banked right and angled upward even more. My pace slowed to a crawl. I stood up in the saddle and thrust my weight into each pedal. Sweat dripped off my nose, and wet hair dribbled onto the inside of my sunglasses. My lungs ached and I panted uncontrollably. I tried to keep pushing and not to think about anything but getting home, but my body just wouldn't go. The air was too thin and the difference was just too great on such an incline. I stopped and got off about half a mile from my home, gasping for air while hanging over the bike. I walked the rest of the way.

A week later I tried it again and the heaving, panting, and aching returned almost as quickly. But this time I was better prepared. I pushed myself harder, dug in deeper, and endured more. I made it five hundred feet farther than the last time. But this time I decided not to walk the remainder of the hill. Once I had caught my breath and finished off my water, I got back on the bike and forced myself to ride the last quarter mile up the steepest portion.

On my third attempt I decided firmly that I was going to ride to the top no matter what. Within minutes the same aches, panting, and profuse sweating returned. I imagined how great it would feel to ride up to the house without stopping. When I felt a twinge of doubt in my mind, I stomped it out. By the time I reached the spot I had rested at the last time, I was exhausted. I reached a flat area and circled on the bike for a few moments to catch my breath without getting off. After a brief respite I turned uphill to tackle the last quarter mile. I panted, wheezed, dripped, and ached. My legs begged me to stop, but I pushed on. Within a few moments I reached the heavenly flat street of my home. I had done it.

I was learning how to push myself beyond my physical abilities. I was learning the edges of my strength. I was learning the value of mental training. For me, the secret was not simply to overcome doubt but to never let it get a foothold in the first place. I needed to train my mind never to give me an excuse to quit. It was a valuable lesson, one I hoped to apply on Kilimanjaro someday.

Lisa and I stayed in Tahoe for a full year, enjoying every season surrounded by the lake and the mountains. I was offered a job in Germany the next spring. We were disappointed to leave our mountain retreat, but we had always wanted to live abroad. It was an opportunity of a lifetime, and we just couldn't resist.

Before we left the United States, Lisa and I needed one last hurrah. We decided to do a ten-day backpacking trip around the northern area of Yosemite National Park. We

Saying goodbye to Yosemite

wanted to soak in the beauty one more time and explore an area where few people roamed. We teamed up with our two friends Stephen and Dennis, the best friends any outdoor adventurer could ever have. Hanging out with these two is like being with John Muir and James Bond at the same time. Stephen, the John Muir of the pair, is the quintessential minstrel poet. He supports himself by cleaning a few houses a week, thus freeing him up to wander in the woods, write poetry, sing opera, and play computer games. Dennis, the James Bond of the duo, is a self-professed gear fiend. He carries with him collapsible titanium chop sticks and owns eight different varieties of stoves, five sleeping bags, several tents, and every Tour de France DVD Lance Armstrong was ever featured in. Or at least that's how much gear Dennis used to have. After hearing our stories of Tanzania, he dug through his impressive pile of outdoor paraphernalia and generously donated several warm sleeping bags, jackets, pants, and even a few pairs of boots to the Kilimanjaro Porters Assistance Project.

It was with these two gentlemen that Lisa and I wanted to venture into Yosemite. Unfortunately, Lisa hurt her foot on a training hike in the Carson Iceberg Wilderness, so the three of us were forced to venture forth without her. One early July morning we started across Tuolumne Meadows, surrounded by brilliant wildflowers, lush green grass, and a clear blue sky. We followed the Tuolumne River past beautiful mountain lupine, through forests of Jeffrey pine and white fir. The trail took us north into unknown territories of the park, into great-sounding places like Matterhorn Canyon, Saw Tooth Ridge, and Slide Mountain.

We spent the first two days hiking over snow-covered mountain passes and across deep green valley meadows. Then, near the end of the third day, we marched into a damp valley and were attacked by a massive swarm of mosquitoes. They snipped at every speck of open skin, crawled on our faces, up our noses, and into our ears. They stung and sucked faster than we could swat them and our repellent had no effect. We hiked as fast as we could but there was no escape. When we couldn't go any farther, we dropped our packs, pulled out our sleeping bags, and jumped in before we were consumed. But even that wasn't enough. With only our mouths exposed, the hordes still tormented us, forcing us to put towels over the airholes in our mummy bags.

The swarm was still there the next morning. We could find no peace from the horrible bloodsuckers. After two days and nights of this, Dennis had decided he'd had enough. He woke up, jumped out of his sleeping bag, snatched up his belongings, and within seconds took off down the trail.

"I'll eat on the way," he shouted back to us. "I just can't take these fucking mosquitoes anymore!"

Stephen and I decided we needed the calories and ate a proper breakfast while trying to swat the bugs away. We packed up our things and managed to catch up with Dennis a few miles down the trail. Dennis is not what I'd call a power walker. He's more of a steady-Eddie type— much like Lisa in this regard. But the mosquitoes propelled him down the path at a rate I had never seen him take. Unfortunately, his speedy pace had a cost. As the day progressed, Dennis became slower and slower. He stopped to rest more and more frequently and began to complain constantly, not a common trait for Dennis. After a few miles of this I was frustrated. I couldn't understand why Dennis had become so slow and so whiney.

"Are you okay?" I demanded.

"Yeah," he said, flopping on the ground for a rest and a good sigh. "I just hate these mosquitoes."

"Well, you've got to keep moving to avoid them," I suggested.

Stephen was the more compassionate and patient one. He silently hiked behind Dennis, took some of Dennis's gear, and encouraged his partner as best he could. As the miles passed, though, I could see Dennis was crumbling. He was demoralized that he couldn't make his body move the way he wanted it to. I was confused: How could a man who biked thirty miles every weekday and fifty-plus on weekends be so slow and so tired?

I finally figured it out. Dennis wasn't being lazy or weak—he had "bonked." He had burned more calories than he had taken in over the past few days and his body was slowly collapsing around him. No amount of will power was going to fix it—it was pure physiology. We had eaten quick meals while swatting mosquitoes or skipped food altogether and rushed down the trail. Dennis's burst of energy in the morning and lack of breakfast were the last straws. His body was rebelling. He was exhausted, and I was an idiot for not seeing it sooner.

We found a small clearing by the side of a creek where a cool breeze blew through the trees and kept many of the mosquitoes at bay. Stephen and I dropped our gear and forced Dennis to drink a full liter of water and eat as much food as he could. Once he was full, we just sat with our legs in the cool creek and relaxed. The sun warmed our skin and the fresh breeze blew away our impatience and ambition. Behind us was a small field of lupine and white fir trees. In front of us the stream glistened in the afternoon sunlight. The flowing water washed off the layers of mosquito repellent, dirt, and grime from five days of hiking. Suddenly we weren't rushing anywhere. We weren't frustrated by the mosquitoes or worried about how much farther we had to go before finding a decent place to spend the night. Sitting and relaxing by the river was exactly what the trip was supposed to have been. And it was marvelous.

Finally, when we were all feeling better, we packed up again and hit the trail. The mosquitoes still attacked us, which was eternally frustrating, but our pace slowed and we tried to enjoy the rest of the trip. We hiked along high peaks and into deep valleys. We stood at the top of each mountain pass, sometimes for hours, feeling the playful breeze flow through our hair and soaking in the magnificent views. In short, we came to love the experience again. But we needed to be broken first. We needed to be purged of our impatience. Only then could we truly be in the wilderness.

On Kilimanjaro I had been physically broken and in Yosemite it was Dennis's turn. It wasn't his fault that his body quit. It happens. The body's abilities are finite. Yet I still wasn't able to allow myself the same excuse for my failure on the mountain. The Yosemite trip was a rousing success and a great way to say good-bye to Dennis, Stephen, and Yosemite before leaving the country.

It was time to go; Germany was waiting.

Weil im Schoenbuch, our hometown in Germany

8

German Training

Germans love to hike. I knew this before moving to Germany because whenever I hike or camp in the United States, I almost always run into a German. Every time I scale a mountain, a German is already on top, taking pictures and smiling broadly. Turns out, they do this at home as well.

Lisa and I found an apartment in a small town in the southwestern corner of Germany, just outside of Stuttgart. One block away, in front of us, was a vast array of fields full of rapeseed's blooming golden flowers. A block behind us was a sprawling forest that went on for miles, with an extensive trail system throughout. On Sundays all the stores were closed in our little corner of Germany. Lisa and I were amazed how quiet it was on this day of rest. The streets were deserted. We assumed everyone was at home watching soccer or at church. One day we decided to do some exploring in our local forest. As soon as we entered the wooded realm, we saw where everyone was. The forest was packed with hiking Germans. Couples walked together hand in hand. Older people walked with friends. Younger ones walked with dates. Families walked with kids. Even dogs joined the fun.

Germans have made walking into a sport they call Nordic walking. Apparently this is different from regular walking, but I'm not quite sure how, aside from the new set of clothes one must purchase. We saw entire troops of Germans with their leggings, sneakers, breathable jackets, gloves, and Nordic walking poles. Gaggles of women and roving groups of men would march across the fields and into the woods, chucking along with their trekking poles and tight pants.

To enhance the experience, the Germans have strategically placed huts throughout their forests. These huts are actually family restaurants where people can sit in the sun and enjoy a full meal, eat ice cream, and of course drink lots of beer. Some huts even provide lodging for the more adventurous. "Hut-hopping" is a national German activity. They walk for several kilometers (have to go metric, we're in Europe now) and then sit down for a beer or few. Everyone does it, young and old.

Lisa and I became infected with the local pastime as well. Any time we had a free hour or two, we'd walk.

"What would you like to do today?" I'd ask Lisa.

"How about a walk in the woods?"

"You don't want to walk in the fields today?"

"No, I walked in the fields yesterday."

"Do you want to walk in the woods behind the house?"

"No, I walked there the day before. Let's walk in the woods across the road." Then we would put on our appropriate gear and head out to join the Germans. The more we walked, the more I yearned to be in the outdoors and the more my mind wandered back to Africa.

It had been two years since Kilimanjaro, and doubt had seeped deeper and deeper in me. The further the mountain receded from me, the more I began to wonder if I could have gone farther. The more people I spoke to who had climbed it successfully, the more I wondered what I had done wrong. My failure became this constant itch in the back of my mind, an ache that never fully went away. I might get busy enough with work, family, or fun to lose sight of it for a while, but it would come back: Why didn't I make it when so many others did?

The day I came off Kilimanjaro I suspected I would have to return one day. I needed to find out if I really had it in me. Unexpectedly Germany gave me the opportunity. It's a lot closer to Tanzania than California is, so the airline tickets were much cheaper, and in Germany you get six weeks of vacation every year. It doesn't matter if you've been with a company for ten days or ten years—six weeks vacation! Clearly this was a civilized country.

I decided to run the idea past my friend Tim, the owner of Sierra Wilderness Seminars. Lisa and I had climbed Mount Shasta with his company, and he and I had kept in touch since then. I knew Tim was interested in checking out Kilimanjaro himself, and when I shared my thoughts with him, he immediately volunteered to join me.

"Tim, I've just got to know if I can make it," I explained.

"You just need to fill your buckets," he replied.

"My buckets?"

"Yeah, the way we think about it, we all have three buckets: our physical ability to adjust to altitude, our physical strength, and our mental strength. It sounds like your body doesn't adjust well to altitude; it's a small bucket. There isn't anything you can do about that, it's just your own physiology. So you've got to make sure you compensate by filling your physical and mental strength buckets even more."

"Yeah, but I was fine on Shasta and didn't have any real problems until the summit," I protested.

"Everybody's different, Dan. I have trouble above 18,000 feet. Others have problems even lower than you."

Tim had simply and eloquently put my entire Kilimanjaro experience into perspective. Even before I had started the climb, I was operating from a deficit. By failing to train hard and assuming my natural endurance would carry me up the mountain, I had failed to fill my mental and physical buckets enough to make up for my own limitations above 15,000 feet. Needless to say, I wasn't going to let that happen again.

Tim invited a group of clients and friends to come along while I convinced my old college roommate, Mike, to join us. He was so excited about the idea that he accidentally lured his father into coming as well. Mike's dad is a retired IRS auditor who has run the New York Marathon four times. He had taken to his retirement with gusto, truly enjoying his time to work on the house, play with his grandkids, and do other projects. But most of the house repairs were done and he needed a new project. He overheard us talking about Kilimanjaro and settled on that as his next adventure. Lisa opted not to climb again, but with all these people on board, I couldn't back out. Like it or not, ready or not, I was returning to Kilimanjaro.

We planned to start our climb in early January, just after New Year's. Lisa and I had ascended via the Machame Route, but in the intervening years, it had become just as popular as the Marangu Route (aka the Coca-Cola Route). Because we wanted to stay away from the crowds, we eventually settled on the Rongai Route. I hadn't been to that side of the mountain and was curious to explore something new.

Now it was time to train.

This go around, my training had to be more intense and more consistent. I had learned from Tim and my backpacking trip in Yosemite with Dennis and Stephen that the best way to train was just to walk, a lot. Weight lifting or exercise machines were really no substitute. And so I walked.

Every morning I got up before sunrise and walked ten kilometers (just over six miles) to work. I would wander through the neighboring golf course and past a tiny family farm as the sun rose over the nearby fields. The road cut through a small town and I passed clusters of young children on their way to school. The last few miles meandered through a forest that ended a short distance from work. It was a great way to start the day.

I listened to German language CDs to maximize my time. As I strolled down the path, I talked to myself and practiced my German.

"*Guten morgen,*" the lady's voice would say into my ear.

"*Guten morgen,*" I would reply aloud to no one.

"Good morning."

"*Guten morgen.*"

"Now we will practice the German sound *ach* and *ooch*. For example . . ."

I wandered through the forest making guttural German noises that sounded like I was trying to expel a large hairball. I can't imagine what the local residents thought.

The trail to my office was relatively flat, though, and I needed some hills and longer distances. So on weekends I drove to the Black Forest and trekked fifteen kilometers up long sloping hills surrounded by tall pine trees and the infrequent old castle. Every week I hiked down trails and up mountain passes, rain or shine. But I was surprised to learn that the mental aspect was the most difficult. On Saturdays I would wander alone in the forest all day. The early winter drizzle and gray skies sucked away my enthusiasm. Most of the time I was trekking up a muddy trail in the rain, or trying to keep my footing on the frozen dirt as snow fell on my damp head. Initially I couldn't help but think about how much I would rather be at home sipping hot cocoa and sitting in front of the fire with Lisa.

Weekdays were just as tough. I would wake up before sunrise and step out of the house into the cold, dark morning to get to work on time. It took a monumental effort to get out from under our warm down comforter and set my feet on the frigid tile floor each morning. As I pulled on layer upon layer of clothes, I couldn't help but think, "Go on, just go back to bed for another hour. You can drive to work today." But my previous failure haunted me. I would not go back to Kilimanjaro unprepared.

During my first handful of walks my mind would wander after an hour. I wondered if it was necessary or worth it to hike for so long, to hike in the rain, to hike while Lisa waited patiently at home. But over the course of a few months, I saw changes. As my legs got stronger and more adept at walking, my mind got stronger and more adept at blocking thoughts of failure. As I had learned while biking up that steep hill in Tahoe, the trick wasn't to think about quitting and then choose not to quit. The trick was never to consider quitting in the first place. After a month of training, I woke in the morning on reflex and got up. I didn't lie there thinking about how warm and comfortable my bed was and how cold and wet it was outside. I just went.

Many climbers have told me that mental strength is the most important asset in reaching the summit. I was beginning to understand that. I had always thought that mental strength was something a person was born with or slowly acquired over a lifetime. But I could sculpt it. I was training my mind to go without ever questioning, to just keep going. Every morning I stepped out into the cold, wet darkness, I was getting mentally tougher.

After I had spent more than two months of trekking around my southwestern corner of Germany, my friend Mike and his father, Gerard Davis, arrived. They spent a few days getting over jet lag, enjoying the local sights, and preparing for Africa. We talked for hours about the climb, the mountain, Africa, and our gear. Mike's dad was a meticulous planner and packer (did I mention he was an IRS auditor?). He questioned every piece of equipment he had or didn't have. Mike's preparation was more relaxed. He forgot several items or brushed off the need for others.

"I can always get it there or borrow it from someone," Mike said.

"You realize you're going to Africa, don't you?" I pestered him. "They don't have camping stores or huge grocery stores or many of the things you are thinking of. They don't even have an ATM in Moshi."

"Come on. Of course they have an ATM. I'll just get money out there."

Mike had traveled extensively and had the same attitude I did before my first trip to Tanzania. I found myself worrying about my travel companions constantly. I felt like it was my job to take care of them. It wasn't, of course, but I was getting anxious as our departure approached and it made an excuse for my anxiety.

On New Year's Eve we sat in a pub in my tiny German town. We raised our beer steins and toasted to our future success: "To the mountain." We clinked the immense glasses and sipped our beers in silence as Kilimanjaro loomed in the distance.

Our guide leads us up Kilimanjaro . . . again

9

There, and Back Again

The plane hummed as we flew over the African continent. Looking down over the Sahara, I was hypnotized by the vast brown desert stretching across the earth for miles below. The sun was setting and the filtered rays of light cast long shadows off what looked like sand dunes from 35,000 feet up. But they could have been mountains, as there was nothing to lend the landscape any scale. The earth glowed red in the twilight, and I couldn't help but repeating in my mind: *I'm going back to Africa!*

Lisa had made plans to meet us a week later in Moshi, after our climb. Mike and Mr. Davis relaxed a few rows behind me as the continent below was swallowed up by the night. Our plane tilted forward and descended toward the now black earth. As we approached, small dots of distant fires began to appear and eventually the runway lights. The plane rolled along the airstrip. There was nothing out there, just miles of shadow. Three years ago my feet had touched the continent for my once-in-a-lifetime adventure. Now I was back to get it right.

The cabin door opened and fresh air swept through the 747. The smell of campfires and diesel filled my senses while the heat of the day's sun radiated off the warm surface below. I had an immediate and overpowering feeling of coming home. But Kilimanjaro Airport was nothing like Nairobi's airport. Nairobi's impersonal, industrial concrete complex was replaced by Kilimanjaro's open runway and small-town terminal. We wandered in the darkness across the exposed tarmac to the tiny lit building. Ours was the only flight that night, and we had the passport control area to ourselves. The local officials seemed almost jovial as they greeted the new arrivals.

By the time we got to the hotel, the same hotel that Lisa and I had stayed in years ago, it was shrouded in silence. We checked into our sparse room exhausted and ready for sleep. Our climb would start first thing in the morning and we needed all the rest we could get. I crawled into bed, pulled the mosquito netting around me, and set my alarm for 8:00 AM.

"Shouldn't we get up earlier?" Mr. Davis asked. "She said the bus would be here at 8:30."

"The bus won't be here at 8:30," I explained.

"But if it comes, we won't have time for breakfast. She said breakfast was over at 7:30."

"I think we misunderstood her. I'm sure breakfast goes longer than that."

"I'd prefer to wake up at 7:00 AM."

"Yeah, I think that's probably better," Mike added.

"Okay," I gave in. "I'll set it for 7:00 AM."

Mike and I settled in as Mr. Davis continued to scrounge around in his pack.

"Can't find something, Dad?" Mike asked.

"I just want to organize my pack for the morning." He had pulled everything out of his duffel bag and dumped it on the floor.

"I thought you did that at Dan's house."

"I want to make sure everything is ready." Mr. Davis continued to rustle on the floor. I don't know how long he did this or if the conversation continued. I fell asleep in seconds.

We woke at 7:00 AM, took a cold showers, and wandered out to the dining pavilion to discover we were the only ones up. We sat in silence and ate our breakfast of warm eggs and cool toast. We were sipping our tea when Tim appeared. He and most of his group had arrived the day before. They'd been exploring the hotel and the town of Moshi.

"We've got a great group," Tim said, beaming. "We're going to have a blast. We had the briefing last night. Man, it's going to be awesome." He had brought with him seven clients and friends. Tim really was the perfect mountain guide, and I was glad to have him along. His enthusiasm was infectious.

But by 8:30 the only people active and out of bed, aside from us, were the punctual Germans. They were all ready, lined up with their packs at the hotel entrance and waiting for their climb bus or safari jeep to take them off on their adventure. The transportation, as I had predicted, had not yet arrived. The Americans and others slowly started to emerge. As the Germans sat on their packs waiting by the gate, everyone else enjoyed a leisurely breakfast and some morning conversation. Mike and I used the time to lock up the extra gear we didn't need while on the climb.

I spotted a familiar face at the hotel entrance. As soon as he saw me, Lawrence greeted me with a broad smile.

Lawrence was the hotel's bellman and had helped Lisa and me immensely during our last visit.

"Hello, Daniel," he said. "How are you?" He grabbed my hand and pumped it like my uncle.

"I'm great, Lawrence. How are you?"

"Oh fine, fine. And how is Lisa? Is she with you?" I had seen Lawrence for only a few minutes over two years ago. And yet he greeted me as if we were family and had just seen each other at the last reunion.

Wandering back across the compound, I ran into Patience, who staffed the hotel's front desk, and shared a similarly warm greeting. This was what I loved about Tanzania. This is what made it feel like home.

By 9:30 AM our bus had finally arrived and we were ready to board. We were making our last-minute checks when our guide appeared. I turned around and there stood the one-and-only Mohamed, my guide from the last trip. His stocky form was planted before me.

"Hello," he said, as chatty as ever. "How are you?"

"Hello, Mohamed," I said, grinning as I shook his powerful hand. "How are you?"

"Fine, fine," he replied.

"We're going to make it this time," I said with confidence.

"Yes, yes. This time we make it."

Mohamed and I filed into the bus and found our seats. It jerked out the hotel gate and started down the dirt road for the northern side of the mountain and the Rongai Gate. I stared out the window taking it all in. I hadn't seen any of this for over two years, and it felt wonderful to be back. Young children ran after the bus screaming "*mzunga!*" and waving. Women sat by the side of the road selling fruit off sheets of plastic. Men pedaled bicycles piled five feet high with coal or massive five-gallon jugs of water. Nothing had changed. Moshi had been permanently preserved for my nostalgic return.

But I could already feel that this trip was different. I wasn't a first-time visitor trying to find my way around. I knew what to expect and understood the challenges before me. And I found being the veteran of the group daunting. Mike, Mr. Davis, Tim, and his clients would look to me for guidance. They expected Tim and me not only to know what to do, but also to perform. The pressures of that reality started to sink in as we approached the mountain.

The bus jostled past fields of sunflowers, forests of banana trees, and the infrequent simple homes. Kilimanjaro stood to our left as we circumnavigated to the northern side. I sat in the back of the bus with Patricia and Paul, a friendly and energetic couple from San Francisco. Patricia was an intense, semi-pro triathlete, a trainer, and a coach. She had cropped blond hair, dark sunglasses, and biceps that looked like she could lift a small elementary school. Paul was a strategy consultant for information-technology companies. He had spent the past six months training and running three marathons. Suddenly my training regimen didn't seem that impressive. Paul had obviously filled his mental and physical buckets.

Eventually we stopped at a little village and filed out into the town center. The hot sun beat down on a dusty square surrounded by a few wooden buildings. Mohamed handed out our box lunches, and we crammed under the shade of the lone tree to eat the ubiquitous chicken, cheese sandwich, and fruit lunches. Later, as we passed through another small town, the bus slowed down. From out of nowhere a gang of men jumped aboard before the bus had even come to a full stop. I looked up in surprise and saw Mik's smiling face, my porter from the last trip.

"*Hu jambo*," I said, using the local greeting.

"*Jambo*," he replied with a grin.

The Rongai Route is on the northern, Kenyan, side of the mountain. It took us more than three hours to arrive, and we were the only group there. Just like last time there was a group of men waiting around for work. But this time they were all coming with us. No one would come all the way to this remote village if he didn't already have the promise of a job. I saw Juma, Patrice, and Ally again—all of whom were part of Mohamed's support team. Juma spotted me, nodded his head and smiled, and returned to his work. Our bags were organized and crews descended on the supplies to prepare everything for the seven-day journey.

The group of climbers signed into the logbook and took pictures of the tiny town, the sign, the mountain, and each other. We stood around talking and waiting for more equipment to arrive. I took advantage of the respite to meet two more members of the group, Rob and Jim. Rob wrote cartoons for the children's cable network Nickelodeon. His broad smile filled his bearded face and his belly almost jiggled when he laughed at his own jokes. Jim was an account manager for online advertising at Yahoo. He was younger and fitter than Rob. They had worked together in the past and had climbed Mount Whitney with Tim's company.

As I met the other climbers, I realized I was actually enjoying the wait, the slow pace forced on me. I was adjusting to Africa again. I accepted that we would leave when we would leave, and wait when we would wait. I chatted for a moment with another member of the group, Carolyn. She was one of the younger climbers, with shoulder-length blond hair and a warm smile under her dark sunglasses. Before coming to Kilimanjaro, she had spent almost a month in Thailand trekking at high altitudes. It was great preparation for this mountain.

A truck rumbled up the hill to us and stopped in a cloud of dust. The tents flew off the back and Mohamed directed the porters in a flurry of activity. Within minutes he had shoved Mik up the mountain and pushed us behind him. It was finally time to leave. The trail started as a dirt road passing short wooden homes cobbled together and ringed by a field of corn. A group of young children came out and waved to us as we passed up the trail. A man working in the field with a sickle paused at the sight of us.

After sitting around for so long, the group was anxious to get moving. Everyone hurried to file in behind Mik and speed up the mountain. But Mik had different orders. He enforced a slow, steady pace, calmly meandering along the trail and forcing everyone to reset to East African speed. As we ambled up the trail, porters passed us with massive loads of tents, food, and backpacks. After a mile or so in the open, cultivated area near the village, we entered the rain forest. This trail was easier than what I recalled of the Machame Route; it was dry with no roots tangling our boots. The rain forest canopy hovered overhead but refused to completely close, allowing in ample light to see and enjoy the trail. We marched along behind Mik through the brush and trees for more than an hour, taking repeated breaks to moderate our pace. Finally we emerged from the jungle and crossed a little creek. Mik made us take another break, and we sat on the large rocks as the water trickled down the mountainside. A few porters arrived from up the trail to collect water.

"I think I can see the camp," someone yelled.

Everyone abandoned Mik and shot up the trail. Being that close, I decided to relax instead and wash up in the cool waters of the creek. Mik's strategy had been to go slow and give the porters enough time to set up our tents and prepare the site for our arrival. I was content to take my time and give them their space. Eventually I wandered up the trail to Camp 1, sometimes called Nalemuru or Simba Camp, at 8,700 feet. Mohamed was already there and directing the porters. Everyone had peeled off and gone to their individual tents when Juma approached with his ever-present smile and two pails of water.

"Water for washing," he said before wandering back.

Mr. Davis walked up to the steaming pail. "What's that for?"

"For washing," I replied.

"What do I need to do that for? I'm just going to get dirty again, aren't I?" Fortunately, Mr. Davis had his own tent for the duration of the trip.

As the sun kissed the horizon, we sat down for dinner in the open air. A long table was set with china plates, silverware, and glass coffee cups.

"This is real luxury," Tim exclaimed. "I've never had this kind of comfort on one of my own trips."

We sat in the cool evening drinking our tea and eating our way through the various courses. The stars slowly appeared as we sat in darkness admiring the night and conversing about everything. As the group relaxed, the topics jumped from camping gear to politics, from adventures to relationships. Somehow we even ended up discussing Rob, the cartoon writer, and his sleeping with fuzzy animals (I didn't try to understand).

As the temperature dropped, the cold drove us to take cover in our respective tents. Mike and I shared a tent. I slithered into my cozy sleeping bag and relaxed in the nylon cocoon. The cool mountain air seeped into the tent and I could feel my heart beating as it tried to adjust to the higher altitude. It felt great to be back outdoors again, to be camping under the stars with Mike. He used to visit Lisa and me in San Jose and we would dash off to the mountains for adventure. But it had been more than two years since our last trip, and I was realizing how much I had missed our outings together.

I faded off to sleep, happy and warm. As the night drifted on, I slumbered in a blissful catatonic state. Then I heard something outside, something my sleeping brain couldn't quite make out. But slowly the sounds began to make sense.

"Mike . . . Mike?" I heard.

"Yeah, Dad," Mike replied from deep inside his sleeping bag.

"What time is it?"

Mike rustled around for a moment. "It's 4:00 AM, Dad." And everything went silent again.

The next morning I emerged with the sun. I stumbled over to Mr. Davis. "Don't you have a watch?"

"No," he replied. "I never need one."

"But you needed one at 4:00 AM," I retorted.

"No, I didn't," he said, smiling. "I just had to ask someone."

The flat top of Kilimanjaro rose before us, wearing a thin shawl of white snow. Glaciers covered the gray, ruffled lava formations that riddled the side of the formation. The sky was clear and we could take it all in. Off to our left, Mawenzi could be seen over the shrubby ridge. A small cloud formation washed up the back side of the lava spires and dissipated as it tried to claim the top.

Slowly everyone came to the table for coffee, tea, and breakfast. Juma dropped off the massive bowl of porridge, and Mr. Davis and I dug in immediately. Next he served the plates of eggs, cool toast, hot dogs, and fruit. I ate my egg sandwich just as I had on my first trip. We packed our things and headed out by 9:00 AM. The trail rose gently before us, surrounded by dry brush and deep blue sky. We hiked through the heather area, and the sides of the trail were lined with sweet-smelling sage. The flora seemed to extend for miles, with the trail being the only break in the dense vegetation. The path itself was in pristine condition, better maintained than some roads I'd been on. I knew this side of the mountain was less traveled than others, but the trail felt as though it had been put here just for us. We trekked up the mountain in glorious solitude, not another soul in sight.

We set off piled up behind Mndeme, our second guide, with Mr. Davis right on his heels. Mndeme was younger than Mohamed and had a genial and open nature about him. He was fond of laughing and seemed to enjoy getting to know the group. He was constantly asking people questions, and his broad smile lit up his face as he engaged each individual. Mndeme had agreed to take point and set the pace while Mohamed organized the equipment and followed, bringing up the rear. After an hour or so, the group started to spread out on the trail. Mr. Davis, Patricia, and Paul were right behind Mndeme. Mr. Davis used him to set pace, and Patricia and Paul went as fast as they could. Mndeme held their competitive speed in check with a slow, steady pace.

Tim wandered along farther back with Carolyn and Carmen. Carmen wasn't so much a client of Tim's as a peer in the great outdoors. She was a U.S. Forest Service peace officer on Mount Shasta where Tim led climbs. She hiked along with her big, dark glacier glasses covering half her face and a broad smile covering the rest. Carmen just loved climbing mountains, and this love emanated from every pore in her body. The Forest Service was the perfect place for her.

"I have authority on any national Forest Service land," she was explaining. "There I can carry a gun and make an arrest."

"*This* is a national forest," Mike pointed out. "Does that mean you're packing right now?"

"No, I didn't want the weight."

Rob and Jim wandered along at a slower pace in the rear, and I decided to stick with them and Mohamed for a while. They seemed like a fun pair, like good after-work drinking buddies.

"What kind of training did you guys do for this?" I asked.

"A lot of 16-ounce curls," Jim answered deadpan.

"Yeah," Rob added. "We've been working on our hydration technique."

They had climbed Mount Whitney with Tim a year ago and were excited to try something harder. But their enthusiasm only went so far. They had done no real training and didn't look to be in great shape. When I thought about Paul running three marathons and these two not doing anything, I wondered if they'd be able to keep up.

We arrived at the second campsite by noon and beat a few of the tents again; the walk hadn't been long enough for the porters to get in front of us. The campsite was located just below a massive ridge of lava that had flowed down the mountain centuries before. On the camp's edge was a large opening referred to as Second Cave. The porters set up their tents and cooking equipment at the mouth of the cave, using it for additional space to sleep. We were on the edge of the heather zone. The brush and bushes thinned out and clumps of grass dotted the area. Small lava rocks poked out of the landscape and made it tough to find a soft, smooth place for our tents.

After lunch we went for a short hike farther up the mountain. We wandered slowly along the trail flanked by tropical-looking giant lobelia and bulbous protea. Farther up, a little stream had cut a thin gorge into the soft lava rock and smoothed the edges away. We were now above

11,000 feet and could feel the difference. The air was thinner and our lungs struggled to take in enough oxygen. No one felt sick yet, but I knew it would come.

To combat the altitude sickness, Mike and his father had started taking Diamox two days before the start of the climb. For the first day they were in the bathroom almost constantly. The prescription label points out that some users might experience blurry vision, tingling in the extremities, and taste alterations. But frequent urination is the most common side effect.

"Do you recommend taking Diamox?" Patricia asked Tim.

"Essentially it tricks your body into thinking there is more CO_2 in your system than there really is," Tim said. "It gets you to breathe more and take in more oxygen."

"It also makes beer taste funny," Carolyn added.

"Really?" Rob asked in obvious alarm. "You mean I might not like the taste of beer when we get back? I can't have that!"

Rob and Jim had started taking Diamox at the base of the climb. Now Patricia and Paul were on the edge of taking it. Was I being foolish to pass on it again? On my last climb I hadn't taken any Diamox because I'd felt fine up to 15,000 feet. But then I suffered on the summit. I understood why Tim and Carmen weren't taking it. They spent a great deal of their time above 10,000 feet. Was I taking an unnecessary risk? I was hungry for the summit, but I also wanted to know I had done it of my own will, on my own power. I thought Diamox would be a crutch for me. I never heard about Everest climbers taking it. So why should I need it on Kilimanjaro?

We sat for over an hour on the smooth rocks by the stream as Tim went on about mountaineering and shared his experiences. Carmen told us about life in the Forest Service. Carolyn told us about her trip to Nepal, her two boys back in California, and what it was like growing up in a commune for the first three years of her life. She was becoming more and more fascinating as we ascended. Back at camp we spent the afternoon lazing. Rob, Jim, and Carolyn played Crazy Eights while the others napped or read. Tim was memorizing the history of the mountain and the various cultures of Tanzania. He was constantly asking questions and seeking out new chances to learn about the country. I felt a bit guilty about my own lack of knowledge. I hadn't brought any books about the mountain, the region, or the flora and fauna. I was proving to be woefully inadequate as an expert.

By the end of the day another small group of climbers had arrived and set up their tents a few hundred feet away from us. We watched them settle in as we huddled in the dining tent. Juma served up warm soup and pancakes, followed by rice, chicken, beans, and a veggie stew. Paul was starting to look tired already and slowly picked at his food. Patricia ate little as well. I worried if they'd have energy for the next five days.

"Are you okay?" I asked.

"We're fine," Patricia replied.

"Are you getting enough calories with just pancakes?"

"I've got some crackers and peanut butter in my tent. Don't worry about me. I really know my body well."

They wandered back to their tent to supplement their dinner with some of their own munchies. The rest of us stayed in the tent sipping tea and staying warm when two young men from the other group approached.

"Hello," one said in a thick Norwegian accent. "Do you happen to know the altitude here? I'd like to calibrate my watch."

"Well, let's see," I said, pulling out my super-duper Lance Armstrong watch. Tim pulled out his own wrist computer and we all compared readings. I consulted our itinerary to get an official statement on what our elevation should be. In the end Lance was closest again.

When we finally called it a night, I snuggled into my sleeping bag and tried to wriggle into a position that didn't include a massive lump of lava rock bulging into my back. I could hear Jim and Rob in their tent discussing the color of their pee and whose pee bottle was whose. Mike drifted off next to me and after a while he, Tim, and someone in Rob and Jim's tent started a chorus of snores. It was like some kind of terrible ensemble of bad instruments being played by their noses. I rolled over and, after much effort, found sleep amid the racket.

At some point the massive internal pressure on my bladder became too much for my unconscious mind and I woke up. It was cold outside and I was pretty darn comfortable in my current location. I rolled over and tried to go back to sleep. I awoke again with the need to pee, and again tried to ignore it and go back to sleep. This is a common game I play when camping. I'm just too comfortable. But eventually my bladder won. My bladder always wins. However, this time I was prepared. I had previously tested my new pee bottle in the safety of my bathroom back home. I was confident that the receptacle was more than adequate for my needs. This time I knew it would work.

I dismissed the lay-down technique I had tried before and immediately wiggled myself onto my knees, still nice and warm in my thick sleeping bag. I brought the pee bottle into the bag with me and positioned it strategically. Then I waited. I tried to force myself to relax and just let nature take over. But it was difficult. The tent was small and even on my knees I had to hunch over. My back was tightening and my neck was kinked by the awkward position.

I hunched there next to my slumbering tent-mate with one hand for balance and the other maneuvering the pee bottle. Suddenly, success. I was in business. Afterward I sealed the bottle, set it outside the tent door, laid down, and slipped back to sleep with a confident smile. I had beaten the bladder. I was becoming a real alpinist.

The next morning the sun shone directly on our tent, waking me, and I emerged to see the glorious mountain. It was cool, the sky was open again, and the summit was crystal clear in front of me. The matted grass under my boots was still damp from the morning dew, and I could feel the cold emanating from the ground beneath me. The tent door opened and Mike crawled out. His face looked awful—his skin had turned beet red, his eyes were hidden in his swollen face, and his lips had inflated to at least three times their normal size. He looked like a baboon in heat and was in obvious pain. He had forgotten to wear sunscreen, lip balm, or a hat the previous day and the sun had punished him mercilessly. Tim was kind enough to give him some lotion to take some of the sting out.

Tim took the opportunity to remind everyone about hydration. "You should be peeing at least five to six times a day," he said. "Clear and copious is the way to go."

Everyone laughed. It wasn't even 9:00 AM and most people had already peed several times. Paul and Patricia were well ahead on their count. Apparently they were up all night going in and out of their tent to relieve themselves in the cold darkness. The Diamox had kicked in.

"I think we're okay on that one," Rob said.

Shortly after breakfast everyone was packed and ready to go. We all stood in a group with our daypacks on, trekking poles ready to go. But we didn't move. Mohamed was busy organizing the porters and shoving them down the trail. We had decided to hike to the Third Cave campsite today, which was only a few miles away. Mohamed wanted to give the porters time to get ahead of us and set up before we arrived. The past two days we had beaten more than half of the porters to the campsites, which was a minor blow to their professionalism and egos. So today Mohamed decided to even the odds for them. We stood, waiting impatiently, when Mike emerged, his face a ghostly, greasy white. He had laid down a full three layers of sunscreen—he was not going to repeat the same mistake.

Finally Mndeme cut us loose and led us out of camp and up the mountain. He set a slow pace with Mr. Davis right behind him, followed by Patricia and Paul. The rest of us filed in after that. The trail cut a clear path through the grassy plain. The soft, sandy grains under our feet made it comfortable and easy to hike. As we ascended, the grass and brush began to thin out. The wildflowers retreated behind us and the black lava rocks and gray gravel began to dominate the landscape.

We hiked for several hours and arrived at the Third Cave campsite shortly after noon. We had climbed to 12,700 feet. It wasn't a huge ascent. In fact, we had hiked more horizontally than vertically. But it gave our bodies more time to adjust to the altitude. On Machame we had gone up to 15,000 feet on the third day before descending back down to under 13,000 feet. The goal had been to work high and sleep low. Here on Rongai we were taking a slower ascent to give ourselves time to acclimate. We sat down for tea and popcorn before lunch was served. The sun was still shining, but clouds were forming below us and slowly enveloping the mountain.

"Can I ask you guys a question?" Paul asked.

"Don't you even . . ." Patricia tried to cut him off.

"Do any of you fold your clothes before you put them in your backpack?" he asked.

"What for?" Tim asked.

"That was my point," Paul replied. "What for?"

"Okay, so I fold my clothes before I put them away. Is that a crime?" Patricia protested.

Given the general lack of use of the washing water by most of the group, and this new revelation that everyone, aside from Patricia, just stuffed their clothes in their packs, I wondered if I wasn't a bit of a prissy outdoorsman. I too folded my clothes when packing my backpack.

Mr. Davis's hands were shaking during lunch as he peeled a hard-boiled egg. Previously he had mentioned that as long as he got to Kibo Camp, he'd be more than happy about his success. I got the impression that he was already feeling weak, even though he didn't show it. His steps seemed smooth and steady, and he was constantly behind Mndeme. In fact, Mndeme had taken to calling Mr. Davis "*Babu*," which is a familiar and endearing form of "grandfather" in Swahili. The nickname was handily taken up by all the porters and guides. Mr. Davis had officially transformed into "Babu of the mountain." Every time someone called him Babu, it seemed like Mr. Davis stood a bit taller, swelling with pride about this new title of honor.

After lunch the clouds enveloped us and it began to rain, forcing us into our tents for shelter. Mike joined Carolyn, Jim, and Rob in their tent for a game of cards while the rest of us went to our own tents. I sat alone as the rain froze and turned to hail. The shower stopped as quickly as it started, and the sun broke through the thick clouds and began to disperse them in large, billowing segments of puffy white crystals. The sun reflected a warm red glow off the top of the clouds, making it look like God himself was shining down on us again and personally pushing them away. It was a beautiful sight. We stood outside our tents staring up at the mountain being revealed to us.

The porters emerged from their tents and went back to work. I thought of my fellow climber Christian telling us on the last trip about the porters who had died from exposure after a sudden rain. Mndeme assured me that everyone was safe and healthy. They prepared dinner while we wandered about the area taking more pictures and enjoying the last rays of sun before the evening.

Dinner was served by 6:00 PM. It was still early and we didn't have much of an appetite yet. But the porters wanted to get dinner done with and cleaned up before it got dark and the cold clouds rolled in again. When Patricia joined us from her tent, she was panting.

"Are you okay?" I asked.

"I was doing crunches," she replied. We were more than 12,500 feet above sea level, hiking several hours each day, and yet Patricia felt the need to add an additional exercise regimen into her daily routine.

"I also brought my bands so I can train on the mountain," she added. "I never travel without my bands."

After dinner Mndeme and Mohamed joined us. Mndeme had a friendly nature, spoke almost fluent English, and seemed to enjoy practicing it. Mohamed, however, seemed like your typical mountain man: strong and reserved. He was not as comfortable with his English, and I frequently wondered if he truly understood me. Mndeme had gradually become the voice of the guides and porters. He and Mohamed would speak in Swahili and decide on a course of action. Then Mndeme would come to us and explain it. Tonight they had decided to stay the next day at the Third Cave Camp, and then hike to Kibo, the summit camp, the following day.

"What is the altitude of the next camp?" Tim asked.

"School Camp is far," Mndeme replied. "It's quite high."

"It's about 15,000 feet," I added.

"So that's almost 3,000 feet," Tim said. "But if we do that tomorrow, we'll have a real easy hike to Kibo Camp, won't we?"

"Yes," Mndeme replied. "Kibo is very close to School Camp. It would only take about one or two hours from School Camp."

Mohamed sat next to Mndeme, nodding his approval at the conversation.

"If we got to School Camp tomorrow, then we'll have plenty of time to rest for the summit ascent right?" I added.

"Yes" Mndeme answered.

"Well, that's probably the best idea then," Tim joined in.

"Yes," Mndeme replied, and Mohamed nodded.

"Okay, so tomorrow we have a tough day and go to School Camp, then a short hike to Kibo the next morning and rest before the summit," I said, summarizing for the group.

"Yes," Mndeme answered. Mohamed nodded.

Within just a few minutes and a couple of questions, we had completely redesigned the rest of the hike. I wondered if our decision had been fully understood by the guides. I repeated it again, this time slower and right to Mohamed. "Tomorrow School Camp, then Kibo. Right?"

Mndeme could see I was checking with Mohamed and turned to him for confirmation. The two chatted back and forth in Swahili for a moment to ensure everyone was on the same page.

"Hmmm," Mohamed grunted, looking back at us.

"Tomorrow will be a hard day," Mndeme explained.

I was concerned about the summit and wanted to do everything in my power to make sure I had all the energy necessary to reach the top. This had been consuming my thoughts. As we climbed, everything I did became directed specifically at the summit, and nothing else. If I ate a lot of food, drank a lot of fluids, took short acclimation hikes—all were to get me to the top. I took pictures and enjoyed the landscape. But I forced down the extra pancake, dumped the additional spoonful of sugar in my tea, and rested my legs to prepare myself physically and mentally for the biggest challenge yet to come.

"Yeah," Tim agreed. "I think we're okay to go higher tomorrow. We've got a pretty strong group. I think it's better to move than just sit here."

"Okay," Mndeme agreed. "Tomorrow we go to School Camp."

With that decision out of the way, we continued to sit around the table chatting. Mohamed listened intently off to the side, trying to discern all the nuances of the conversation. Tim and Mndeme bonded over the business of guiding. Mndeme was thirty-two years old, a father of three. Before becoming a guide, he had previously imported clothes from Kenya, selling them in Tanzania, but the border guards had stopped him and it was becoming a rough business. He decided to turn his English skills to the growing tourism trade and become a mountain guide. He was a porter for one year and followed it with a year as a cook. Then he was an assistant guide for two years before completing his National

Park course and becoming a fully certified guide. Mndeme had been guiding for three years now. Mohamed was forty-three years old and had been a guide for twelve years. Both men looked ten years younger than their actual ages, proof of the health benefits of clean mountain air and exercise. Mohamed was intense and commanding, while Mndeme was friendly and supportive. They made a perfect team on the mountain and complemented each other with their different skills. Mndeme was from the Pari tribe. He explained that few Pari people still lived in the traditional manner. In the past young men were circumcised by the tribal elder or medicine man. Today, however, male babies are taken to the hospital when they are two years old. To celebrate the momentous occasion, the father still frequently slaughters a goat. But the Pari people are modern now, taking regular jobs and working in the fast-paced world of the twenty-first century. Mndeme's brother was working in California. Another tour company had brought him to the United States to help with the business and give presentations. They were up-and-comers now. Even Mohamed, scarcely more than ten years older, seemed like a throwback to a bygone generation.

It was a pleasure getting to spend more time with our guides on this trip. Last time, Mohamed had seemed more aloof, deferring to Christian to share Tanzania with us while he managed the porters and equipment. This time Mndeme was our conduit and easily drew Mohamed into our conversations. I was disappointed when it became too cold and too late to continue and we were forced off to our respective tents for the night. I unzipped the tent door and a thin layer of ice fell from the side, reminding me how cold the mountain really was. My sleeping bag was a warm embrace and within minutes I was fast asleep.

A few hours later I woke with a splitting headache. I pressed my eyes into their sockets and rolled around in my bag trying to think the pain away. But it was relentless. I hadn't drunk enough liquids during the day. The hike had been short and mild and my body hadn't demanded it . . . until now. I groped for my water and forced down the entire liter. I slowly felt the liquid saturate my dehydrated cells. Of course, then I had to get up two more times in the night to pee, but that wasn't much of a bother now that I'd perfected my pee bottle technique.

Signpost on the way to Kibo Camp

We rose to cool sunshine. The tent was freezing and I pulled my warm clothes from the bottom of my sleeping bag and wiggled into them before stepping out into the new day. Carmen was sitting on a nearby rock, soaking in the view. I was no longer amazed to see her out of her tent so early every morning. Carmen hated the cold and frequently wore at least two layers more than anyone else at any particular time. At 7:00 AM she was wearing three layers on her legs and five on her upper body. I took to using her as my barometer. If I didn't know what to wear, I'd just subtract two layers from what Carmen was wearing. Her sensitivity to the cold in no way hindered her pure joy of the mountain. She was always the first one out, basking in the silent early rays of the new day.

After breakfast we headed out for School Camp and by 10:30, the clouds began to roll in and blanket the mountain. The massive white forms advanced up the mountainside and covered the landscape as the cool mass enveloped us. They sucked the warmth and sun from the air and the temperature dropped. Carmen piled on two more layers. Mohamed took the lead and everyone marched behind him in a single line. He forced a slow pace, but no one wanted to push it. Today we were taking the mountain straight on and ascending more than 3,000 feet. The well-worn trail quickly disappeared, and we trekked up the open gravel and scree. The few remaining small shrubs and tufts of grass completely disappeared, replaced by small rocks, gray gravel, and dark sandy dirt. We were now entering the mountain's alpine region. Within a few hours all signs of life were gone; only lifeless earth remained.

Tim and Mndeme brought up the rear of our column, chatting about guiding and the mountain, and sharing war stories about good and bad customers. I could feel the lack of oxygen in my lungs and the increase of lactic acid buildup in my muscles making my legs heavy. But I pushed on with the group. As we got closer to the campsite, Tim conducted a small mountaineering class, teaching everyone how to do the rest step. It's simple really. Between every step, stop and rest. The secret was to rest with my weight on my bones, not my muscles. The goal was to get enough oxygen to keep functioning while using as little energy as possible. Tim and Rob marched in unison to demonstrate. "Step, breathe, rest. Step, breathe, rest." Tim said in coordination with his moving legs. "It's important to breathe all the time," Tim explained. "Most people hold their breath when they sit down, lie down, or do a quick task. Those are the times you get a bad headache and feel dizzy. Every time you stop or sit down, make sure you breathe in and out a few times. Force yourself to do it."

We arrived at School Camp by early afternoon, after almost five hours of strenuous hiking. The ascent had been steep and sandy, requiring a lot of energy as the soft ground gave way under each step. We were now 15,400 feet above sea level and my chest heaved to pull in enough oxygen. Fifteen thousand feet is one of those magic alpine numbers. Something happens to the body at this point that changes the rules of the game. Mount Shasta was only 14,179 feet. It had been hard but manageable. But above 15,000 feet is where the lack of oxygen begins to have a marked impact on performance and function, where the debilitating headaches and nausea can really kick in. All of us could feel it.

Our tents were set up on the side of a steep cliff with massive boulders overhead and an expansive view all the way down the mountain. There was a large hut perched nearby, a rectangular wood frame building with green sheet metal nailed all over the sides and roof for protection. In the civilized world it would have stored hay. Here it was paradise. Jim, Mike, Rob, and Carolyn sat inside at the wooden table and played cards again while waiting for lunch. Tim watched on as they giggled their way through five hands of Crazy Eights.

"I feel like I'm high," Mike said. "Well, at least this is what I've heard it feels like."

"I don't know what the heck is so funny," Rob chuckled. "But it is." Their game had turned goofy from the lack of oxygen. After a while, they gave up playing altogether and just laughed at each other's stupid jokes.

Finally lunch was served in the cozy room while the cold wind rattled at the sheet-metal walls. We hid out in the hut well after our meal, sipping tea for more than an hour while telling silly stories.

My head ached but I forced down my lunch of stew and potatoes. I knew the calories would help, but it was real work keeping it down. After lunch I wandered back to my tent and had a few Tylenol before lying down. We were definitely above 15,000 feet and my body knew it. My altitude bucket was quickly draining.

I emerged from my tent later, feeling a little better. Off to the west I could see the peak of Mawenzi poking through the clouds. The clouds themselves seemed to be almost alive. They opened and closed above and around us, alternating between enveloping us in a cold gray mist and exposing us to the sun's powerful rays. I wandered over to the hut to join the others again. As I passed Patricia's tent, I could see her inside exercising with her bands and doing crunches. Inside the hut I found the rest of the group chatting. There seemed to be no rhythm or reason to the conversation—it slid from politics to religion to camping gear to movies.

Rob was trying to explain his favorite reading genre, medieval mysteries. "It's basically a murder mystery that takes place in medieval times," Rob said.

"That's a genre?" Mike asked.

"Well, I wouldn't say it's really popular, but we do have a small cult following," Rob answered. "Did you ever see the movie *The Name of the Rose* with Sean Connery? Where he's a monk who investigates a murder at a monastery? That's a medieval mystery."

Eventually Mohamed and Mndeme joined us in the hut and took a seat next to Tim. Tim was wearing his massive, puffy red down jacket. Mndeme sized up the toasty garment.

"Do you want to try it on?" Tim asked him.

Mndeme's eyes grew large. "Yes." Tim handed him the jacket, and Mndeme climbed into it. By the time he zipped it up, the petite guide disappeared completely. Tim flipped the hood up and all we could see were Mndeme's two eyes peeking out of a small crack in the top of the garment.

"Oh, it's so warm," we heard from inside the red puff pile.

Tim sat shivering in the cold, now much smaller and less protected.

Mndeme asked Tim about his background, what life was like where he lived, and other topics. It wasn't clear if he was generally interested in any of this or was just trying to distract Tim from remembering that Mndeme was wearing his nice warm coat.

"Um . . . can I have my coat back?" Tim finally asked.

"Oh . . . yes." He peeled it off and handed it slowly back to Tim, who immediately pulled it back on and zipped it to the top. Mndeme sat there, now half the size he had been just moments before, looking almost naked.

"That is very nice," he said, sighing.

After dinner we headed back to our tents. It was still early and Mike and I sat in our small nylon home chatting as we lay in our sleeping bags. In the quiet of the night we could hear the whispers of conversations around us.

"Well, I wouldn't tell," Rob announced in the tent next to ours, his loud voice booming among all the whispers.

"What do you think that's all about?" Mike asked in a whisper.

"I don't know, but I'm damn curious now," I whispered back. We lay as still as possible and held our breath to better discern what was happening in the tent beside us.

"It's the international rule," we heard Carolyn say. "Don't you know the international rule?"

"I don't think so," Jim replied.

"Whatever happens abroad stays abroad," she explained. "It doesn't count."

Mike turned to me. "Did you know that rule?"

"No, first time I've heard it."

"Yeah, the international rule," Rob joined in, his boisterous voice jumping out again in the quiet of the night.

Then there were more whispers. It was getting juicy now and we were curious how it would end. We knew Jim had a girlfriend back home. Apparently that point was causing some problems and his fellow climbers were more than willing to help him work through the issue.

"Can you make anything out?" I whispered.

"No," said Mike.

It was Carolyn and Jim talking now. They were discreet enough to keep their voices down.

"Well, I've got to pee," Rob announced with his characteristic volume and grace. We heard him step out of the tent and stomp away, whistling as he disappeared into the night.

With that, the tent next to us went silent—no more whispers, hushed tones, mumbles, or discussion of any kind. The night turned soundless except for Rob's scuffs in the distance as he wandered over to the hut. The drama appeared to be over and the international rule, as stated by the Geneva Convention, had apparently prevailed. Freedom had been victorious and travelers everywhere rejoiced at another mountain romance blooming, at least that's what Mike and I suspected. With that happy thought, I drifted off to sleep.

I woke at 6:30 AM. The temperature in the tent was still below freezing and I was in no mood to emerge until that changed. The night had been cold and windy, and I had struggled to get more than a few hours of good sleep. My head ached and I was feeling anxious about the summit. I started to relive my previous climb and remembered the nausea, the headache, and the freezing cold. I wondered if I had what it would take this time to make it to the top. My ego pitched in and reminded me that this time, if I failed, it would be in front of Mike, his seventy-three-year-old father, and all of these fellow climbers.

As I looked at Mawenzi, I was reminded again that Hans Meyer and Ludwig Purtscheller had actually climbed those pointy crags after they had summited Kilimanjaro for the first time ever. Mawenzi is a more technical and dangerous climb by far. Today one can summit Kilimanjaro with nothing but a good pair of boots and a warm jacket. Mawenzi requires skill, training, and equipment. In the end those men spent more than sixteen days above 15,000 feet and managed to summit one of the smaller peaks of Mawenzi *in addition to* the Kilimanjaro summit. Here I was trying for my second chance at just the summit, hoping to be back at poolside within a week. Of course, in my defense, it had also taken Meyer two tries.

Mohamed organized breakfast and we sat huddled in the cold hut, sipping tea. Juma brought in his typical enormous pot of porridge. Babu and I dug in immediately; Babu was a big fan of oatmeal, eating it for breakfast almost every day at home. "No one else wants any?" he asked as everyone sat back watching us dig into the off-white mush.

"No more porridge," Carolyn demanded.

Paul just looked into the pot and turned away, unable to bear the sight.

"This stuff is delicious," Babu explained to the weary group. But no one partook, leaving Babu and me three bowls each. We scooped out our servings and piled on the brown sugar crystals. It was exactly what my stomach needed: very simple calories.

Next, Juma served the regular plates of eggs, hot dogs, cold toast, and some vegetables. When he brought in the first few plates, everyone was quick to offer them to anyone else. Many of us were feeling nauseous; not much looked appetizing. Paul couldn't even have a plate in front of him, his face turning pale at the mere sight of eggs. He had been struggling the past few days with diarrhea; he was having a hard time eating anything but the simplest of foods. Yesterday's hike had been tougher than the day before and the drain was evident on his face.

"Are you taking the Diamox pills?" Tim asked.

"Yeah, we've been taking them for a few days now," Patricia answered for Paul.

"Do you have any allergies or anything?" Tim asked. "The sulfur in the Diamox may be what is giving you trouble." Paul nodded at this information but didn't seem to have the energy to contribute to the investigation.

Breakfast was more quiet than usual. No one ate much; everyone was distracted. Finally Patricia broke the silence: "Is anyone else nervous about the summit?"

"Do you realize that you're already higher than many of you have ever been?" Tim tried to encourage the group. But no one seemed in the mood for a pep talk.

After breakfast people meandered back to their tents to pack up and prepare to move to the final camp before the summit. Kibo Camp was relatively close, so there was no need to hurry. We enjoyed the lazy morning and packed under the unusually clear skies.

The group left camp in a single-file line at 9:45 AM. The hike was easy: it traversed around the mountainside across to Kibo Camp. There was no elevation gain, the trail was flat gravel and scree, and it was a short distance. Within an hour we came over a small rocky escarpment and immediately saw Kibo Camp below us. We stopped on an outcropping and took pictures of the landscape from above. Below us the saddle between Kibo and Mawenzi extended for miles in a flat brown plain. The alpine desert was bisected by two thin lines that led off away from Kibo. A group of small dots was making its way up one trail from the Mawenzi Tarn Camp. Another few dots were hiking away from Kibo to descend down to Horombu Camp via the Marangu Route. They had completed their summit attempt and were going home. That would be us in twenty-four hours. Had they been successful, or were they marching off the mountain defeated? My time would come soon enough.

As we hiked down to Kibo Camp, I kept looking up at the summit. It was shortly before noon and the clouds had not yet come in to veil the barren view. I could see everything. The zigzag trail up the steep mountain wall was obvious. A wooden sign embedded in a large stone pile marked the trail: SUMMIT 5–6 HRS.

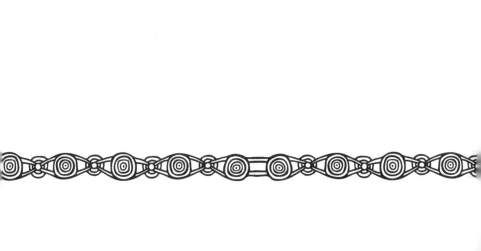

En route to the summit

10

This Time, With Feeling

Our summit climb would begin in twelve hours, but after we had
unpacked and settled in to our new home at 15,340 feet, there
was nothing more to do. No amount of stretching, training,
or crunches would make a difference now. All we could
do was wait. I tried reading, taking pictures, chatting with
my fellow climbers, looking at the scenery, strolling around
the campsite—anything to keep my mind busy. Nothing
worked. So I lay in my tent and stared at the ceiling.

The boredom was relieved in the afternoon by lunch
service. Juma circulated through the tents and called
everyone to the table. Paul huddled quietly over a cup of
tea, his body sagging and his head hanging down almost
into his cup. He had vomited recently and was feeling
worse. He hadn't given up hope and was working hard
to preserve his strength, but he had eaten little over the
past two days and continued to deteriorate the higher up
we went. I was certain he wouldn't summit. Everyone
else picked at the sandwiches and fruit the porters put
out. Mike dumped a pile of energy bars on the table for
everyone to share, but no one had any appetite. We tried

to force down a few calories, knowing we would need them later, but it seemed like a lost cause. I settled on sugary tea.

The conversation was less animated than before. Carmen and Tim were the only chatty ones. Mike threw in a few of his off-color Brooklyn jokes to break up the mood, but the rest of us sat there mute, our thoughts focused on what lay ahead. The discussion turned to the upcoming climb and people shared thoughts and strategies for clothing, water, food, and anything else that crossed their minds.

"You'll want to have some quick-energy food where you can easily get to it," Tim instructed. "You won't want to stop and dig through a backpack or anything like that. Keep it in your jacket pocket. You'll want the calories."

"Should I bring any Diamox with me?" Carolyn asked.

"It wouldn't hurt," Tim answered.

"Yeah, but what's it going to do for you at that point?" I piped in. "Besides, are you really going to want to mess with those tiny pills in the dark?"

"My God, man, it's not the moon!" Tim blasted. "Jeez, it's not that bad up there. Come on."

My face turned red and I flashed with anger. I knew Tim was just joking around, but his shot went deep. I had felt myself getting more irritable as we'd ascended the mountain and as I'd come closer to facing the summit. It was too late for me to take Diamox, and I was only a few hours away from learning if I'd made another huge mistake. Tim's attack on my experience and credibility made me want to deck him. But I chuckled along with the others and then just slumped in my seat, stewing.

Later I stood alone in the afternoon sun, staring up at the mountain. The clouds had not come in yet and the route remained exposed for me to look upon and wonder. Tim came over.

"I guess I'm letting my last experience color too much of my advice," I suggested.

"Yeah," Tim replied. He squinted up at the summit. The Rebmann Glacier crept over the flat top of the mountain, the white ice glistening in the afternoon sun, radiating against the barren rock.

"I guess anything that makes clients feel better and doesn't hurt them is okay, huh?"

"Yeah," Tim repeated. That was the end of the discussion.

I drifted off to my tent for some solitude. I lay on my sleeping bag, feeling both anxious and excited. I dreaded what the mountain had in store for me and the hours of mind-numbing climbing ahead. But I couldn't wait to get out and attack it. A chilling wind blew through the open tent and my body shivered. My mind wandered, observing its own dialogue.

My mind: *"What kind of moron brings eight people with him to climb a mountain he failed to climb successfully before?"*

Me: *"Um."*

My mind: *"Wouldn't it have been smarter to do this successfully alone first?"*

Me: *"Probably."*

My mind: *"Not only that, but you had to bring your friend and his seventy-three-year-old father with you. You know they're going to make it, don't you?"*

Me: *"Yes."*

My mind: *"Well, what are you going to do about it?"*

At about this point, I realized that it was my brain that had gotten me into this situation in the first place. I tried not to listen to it any more. Instead, I tried to settle into a kind of mantra: *Must not fail . . . Must summit . . . Must not fail . . . Must summit . . .*

As this mantra worked its way into my psyche, I questioned it. Perhaps this wasn't the best attitude to have. My focus was completely on *not* doing something. If I was going to accomplish this feat, I needed to be as positive as possible. I started to visualize what it would feel like to reach the summit. I kept seeing the long hike and me strong all the way. I imagined myself standing at the top, flag in hand, claiming this mountain for America (okay, maybe I got a bit carried away).

I tried to force my mantra to change: *I will summit . . . I can do it . . . I will summit . . . I can do it . . .*

This was my internal battle for several hours. By 10:00 that night I couldn't sit still any longer. I needed to get out of my sleeping bag. I needed to get walking. I needed to attack that mountain. Most of all, I needed to relieve my bladder!

Luckily, just when I was ready to burst, Mndeme came by to rouse us. It was time. As everyone began donning their layers, Mike and I arrived at an agreement. The summit deserved something special. It deserved a fresh pair of underwear. We marked the momentous occasion as our mothers had taught us and we changed our underwear. On top of this I layered two pairs of thermal pants and a pair of lined, waterproof-breathable snow pants. On my torso I wore two thermal shirts, a down jacket, a fleece jacket, and a shell jacket. On my hands I had a pair of thin, liner gloves inside thick mittens, and on my head was a knit cap. For my feet I had a pair of silk liner socks, wool socks, boot warmers, and my full-grain leather Gore-Tex boots with Vibram soles. I was not going to get too cold this time! I filled a CamelBak backpack with a sport drink, cinched it down as much as possible, and wore it under the shell jacket to keep from freezing. The water tube snaked under my shell with the mouthpiece popping out at the collar for easy access. By the time I exited my tent, I was steaming.

Tim, Carmen, and Carolyn were already waiting in the darkness. Rob and Jim appeared after a while, and finally Patricia and Paul emerged. Despite his altitude sickness, Paul had decided to try for the summit. I was impressed with his resolve but also a little annoyed. I was certain he wouldn't make it to the top. If so, one of our guides would have to bring him back down safely, leaving one fewer guide to help the rest of us. We huddled in a circle, inspecting one another's gear and clothing choices as we waited for the guides. The waiting began to feel like hours.

"Okay, that's it. I'm getting out of here," Tim announced. He started toward the summit trail.

"I'll go with you," Carmen said and followed.

"Do you think that's a good idea?" I asked the back of Tim's head. "What about the other clients?"

"The guides are coming," he replied with a wave. "I can't stand here any longer."

I was furious. He was abandoning his clients. It seemed uncharacteristically unprofessional of him. He and Carmen disappeared into the dark as the others stared at me.

"We should wait for Mndeme and Mohamed," I said with as much authority as I could muster. "We'll meet those two on the way."

At midnight our guides emerged from the darkness; it had taken over an hour to get everyone ready. We marched to the base of the climb and Mohamed lined us up. He put Babu behind himself, asked for the women next, and finally anyone else who wanted to come along. Above us we could see a few small groups of dancing lights. We were about to join them. Everyone switched on their headlamps and started trudging along the dirt track. It didn't take long for the relatively smooth and well-worn path to pitch upward and transform into scree and sand. An infinite number of switchbacks confronted us.

Slowly we marched up the dirt hill, zigzagging back and forth, back and forth. *Chuck-step, chuck-step* was our rhythm, as we planted our trekking poles and shuffled along. Gradually our snake of light began to wind its way up the mountain. *Chuck-step, chuck-step.* Already it was getting tedious. Reminding myself of Tim's suggestions to focus on a landmark, I looked up the hill, searching for anything that wouldn't make my head spin. All I saw was darkness—except for the boots moving in front of me. They mesmerized me and I grew dizzy watching them. I'm still not sure if my dizziness was from a lack of oxygen or from staring at those boots and the ground beneath them, rolling on for hours on end.

As we plodded along, I became more accustomed to this feeling of being in a dream. I was dizzy and nauseous, but my feet kept moving as if detached from me. I decided that as long as my legs kept taking me forward, I would continue, no matter how uncomfortable it got. As the hours passed, I fell further into my dream-walk drunken state. *Chuck-step, chuck-step.* I was almost starting to enjoy this whole thing.

Suddenly the feet in front of me stopped. I looked up from my stupor and realized we were taking a break.

"It's 2:00 AM," I heard Carolyn say. "Does anyone know our elevation?"

I could have easily looked at my watch to see the time or altitude, but I didn't want to know. The last time I had attempted Kilimanjaro, I had checked my watch constantly and had found the lack of speed and elevation gain demoralizing. This time I had decided that the top was the top. I'd get there when I got there. It didn't matter to me where we were. I just knew we weren't at the summit. I forced down a candy bar and took a few sips of my sport drink. My stomach revolted at the imposition, but I kept it down and began the march again.

Chuck-step, chuck-step. The going was more tedious now. I was comfortable with my new, stoned state but also aware of how slowly we were going. I looked up from time to time and saw Babu at the front of the column, chugging along. "How you doing up there, Babu?" Mike shouted. "Babu of the Mountain! You can do it!"

No one was going to forget that Babu was there, a seventy-three-year-old retired IRS auditor, leading us up the mountain. He provided us ample motivation to go at least as far as he did. Mike's encouragement brought a smile to my face. He and I had previously joked that we couldn't let Babu make it to the top without us. We had made a pact before the climb that, if necessary, we'd tie Babu's hiking boots together and steal his trekking poles. But now that it was real, Mike did nothing but encourage his father. Babu just kept on going, in his zone, oblivious to time and distance.

I tried to emulate his climbing. *Okay, just turn your mind off,* I said to myself.

"Seems like a long way to go," came the reply.

Shut up and go to sleep! Just stop thinking!

"How much money did we pay to do this? Wouldn't Hawaii have been a much better idea?"

Logic has no place on a mountain. Especially at three in the morning and 17,000 feet above sea level, with about 30 percent less oxygen than normal. I couldn't force my mind into that magical zone. I needed a tool. Tim had suggested counting. So I began to count. I hadn't studied my German in weeks, so I thought this would be the perfect chance to brush up on it. *Eins, zwei, drei, vier* . . . I counted in my head to one hundred in German.

Chuck-step, chuck-step. As the tedium and steps lulled my mind, I lost count and had to start over. This happened several times before I finally reached one hundred. But I still wasn't in the magical zone. So I started to count from a hundred down to one in German. This proved to be a lot more difficult than I had anticipated, and by the time I got to one, I decided to forget the whole exercise. It had required way too much concentration and energy.

Chuck-step, chuck-step. I decided to try counting one more time, this time in Japanese: *Ichi, ni, san, shi* . . . I hadn't spoken Japanese in years. As the elevation increased, the oxygen decreased, and the numbers got higher, I kept getting confused and lost. I abandoned this course and changed to English once and for all: *One, two, three, four, five, six, seven, eight, nine, ten* . . . .

The trouble with counting in my native language was that it was too easy. By the time I got to one hundred, I had no idea how I got there or even if I'd hit all the numbers. Had I skipped over a few? How long had that taken? I was just getting into this new internal dialogue when I heard a commotion above. I raised my head to see a group of guides standing around a single client hunched over, sitting on a rock. He must have been from one of the groups that had started before us. The guides argued back and forth, Swahili flashing all around us as the discussion heated up.

"Would all of you just shut the fuck up!" the client blurted out, before collapsing onto the rocks around him. From what I could gather, this client was exhausted and sick from the altitude. His guides had been discussing how best to get him off the mountain. Mohamed stepped forward. He barked out orders, pointed to guides, and lifted the protesting client. He sounded like FDR after

Pearl Harbor, exuding confidence and power. I have no idea what Mohamed said, but it was authoritative and followed by all. He then turned to us. "Okay. Let's go," he commanded. And we went.

At some point Mohamed decided it was time for another break. I looked up from my pensive plodding and saw a large rock in front of us, with Carmen and Tim sitting at the foot of it. We'd finally caught them. Everyone sat down to rest and eat or drink what they had. Both Carmen and Tim were in good spirits and enjoying their climb. I lay on the ground and looked up at the stars. It was a beautiful night sky, almost completely clear. I could see the Big Dipper and followed the ladle to where I would normally expect to see the North Star, which wasn't there. We were two degrees below the equator and couldn't see the North Star from this location. I was comforted to see some other celestial friends like Orion still visible. As I followed the sky down, it was almost impossible to tell where the dark night and shining stars ended, and the dark land and shining lights and fires began. The break between heaven and earth seemed almost nonexistent from Kilimanjaro.

I looked up from my resting spot and could see the faint silhouette of the crater rim far above. It seemed a long way off and not getting any closer. I could see a few small groups groping their way up the hill ahead with their headlamps lighting the way, still far from reaching their goal. Finally we gathered ourselves up and were off, all together this time. *Chuck-step, chuck-step.* I plodded along in my own little dreamworld. I was more nauseous now, but my legs kept working, so I kept going.

I could hear Carmen talking at the front of the line. "I keep waiting for this to get hard," she chuckled. "This really isn't that bad." Her voice was full of energy and enthusiasm, as if she were just walking down the street back in

Mount Shasta, California. A new wave of nausea hit me as I considered what I would do to that cheerful woman if I could only reach her. I satisfied myself with the idea that she probably had a naturally large altitude bucket. The group began to break up. The pace was too slow for Carmen and Tim. They went on ahead with Ally while Mohamed kept the rest of us in tight check behind Babu. Suddenly, after a few more steps, Babu slipped. He reached out, stabilized himself with his trekking poles, and quickly regained composure. In a flash Mohamed grabbed him. He tore off Babu's gloves and inspected his fingers. He shone his light in Babu's eyes and checked his lucidity. He took away Babu's backpack and threw it over his own shoulders. After a few more moments of inspection, he satisfied himself that Babu was still fit, and we continued. Babu told me later that as this inspection was taking place, he was working on his list of reasons why Mohamed should not send him back down the mountain. He was terrified he'd be forced to go back just because of a minor slip. (In Babu's defense he trips at sea level too.)

At our next rest stop I was in the deep throes of nausea and completely out of my head with the dizzy dreamland. My altitude bucket was completely empty and I was digging deeper into my coffers of mental and physical strength. I tried to force down another candy bar, but even the thought of it sent my stomach into the back of my mouth. I contented myself with a sip of my sports drink and a seat on the ground. As I sat there, minding my own business and fighting back the contents of my stomach, Patricia and Carolyn called out to me that the pace was too slow. They wanted permission to go ahead.

"Talk to Mohamed," I replied weakly. I had neither the patience nor the capacity to decide anything. *Chuck-step, chuck-step.* We trudged on. I was hiking alone with

Rob and Babu now. I had no idea where anyone else was, nor did I really care. The trail was pretty obvious at this time (just go up), and there was a long line of clients and guides. So I let myself focus on my own steps. Mohamed and Mndeme would worry about the clients. As I marched, I heard Rob asking, "This is a vacation? Why the hell didn't I go to Hawaii?" I had to laugh. It was typical Rob and a nice break from the reality of our marathon up the mountain. I came upon Mike, slumped on the side of the trail. He sat in the dirt with his arms and trekking pole hanging limp by his side. Surprised to see him there, I realized that I hadn't heard his encouraging voice for a while.

"I'm done," Mike said. "I'm going back down. My head hurts and I can't breathe." His appearance jolted me out of my dreamworld. I could see how hard he'd tried and how deep he'd dug. I checked my altimeter watch: 18,400. Mike had climbed four hundred feet higher than I had on my first attempt—with almost no training and no experience. My only consolation was that he had taken Diamox. My feeble vanity clung to the thought.

"18,400 feet, dude. You did an awesome job! I'm proud of you," I said. After a few seconds, I told him: "I'm going to keep climbing." I had to keep going.

"Okay," he replied. "I'll see you back at camp." Juma helped Mike up and they started down the trail together. Rob and Babu rested against a rock just below me, watching them leave. Rob looked up at me.

"I'll stay with Babu and Mndeme," he said. "This is a good pace for me."

This was Rob's chance to quit if he wanted to. Juma and Mike were giving him an excuse to go down and he was choosing to continue. But now Rob, Babu, and I were left with Mndeme while Mohamed was leading the others well ahead of us. Since the three of us were now sharing one guide, if any one of us needed to go down early, all of us would have to go back together.

"What if Babu needs to go back down?" I asked.

"It wouldn't bother me to have to go down with him," Rob admitted.

I could feel my confidence begin to waver with the thought of going down with Rob and Babu if necessary, going down because of someone else in the group and not me. As the thought of quitting began to form, I felt another part of me jump on it and stamp it out before it could become real.

"I'm going to keep going." I turned around and started trudging up again. That was it. That was the closest I would allow myself to get to choosing or even thinking about quitting. I would climb this mountain. As long as my legs would carry me, I would climb this mountain. I didn't care if I went with other climbers or even if I had a guide or not. I didn't wait for Mndeme to lead me or Rob and Babu to join. There was still a steady stream of people going up the mountain. I joined the line and kept marching.

Rob, Babu, Mndeme, and I reached Gillman Point at 18,650 feet. We had finally ascended the side of the old Kibo volcano and were now standing on the crater rim. There was a tall sign posted on the corner of a small rock ledge to notify everyone how far we'd really come. As we scrambled over the last boulder, we reached it just in time to see the sun explode over the horizon. Its rays spread across the sky and warmed my face. The rocks burst with color as light danced across the top of the mountain. The dark gray world was now illuminated. I could see the mountain all around me. We stood on the crater's rim and looked down inside the now extinct volcano. A few small glaciers clung to the inside, and a fat cinder cone sat in the center with a deep hole in the middle, a reminder of a time when Kibo's fire burned bright.

Although Kilimanjaro is famous for its flat top, it's not exactly level. We had spent the past seven hours hiking up from Kibo Camp to the crater rim at Gillman Point, roughly four miles and four thousand feet of elevation. However, we were not at the mountain's highest point. To get to the peak, at 19,340 feet above sea level, we needed to trek another hour and a half around the crater rim to reach Uhuru Peak.

At least now the trail was more merciful, as it gradually rose along the rim until it reached Uhuru Peak. The hardest part was behind us. Now all we really had to do was walk a gradual incline for less than two miles. As we set off toward the summit, I was filled with renewed energy and enthusiasm. The sun was up and we finally had a view. I no longer needed to stare at the dizzying feet in front of me. I could see all the glory of the mountain.

As far as I was concerned, I had made it. I knew I hadn't reached the summit yet. But I was past the hardest part. The rest was just a short hike around. My step took on a new spring as my enthusiasm and pride brought tears to my eyes.

I made it, Love, I said mentally to my wife, some 5,000 miles away. *I made it.*

The longer we hiked, the more my pep talk at Gillman Point began to wear off. The summit I'd thought was so close seemed to keep getting farther and farther away. I slowed down, the spring in my step fading fast. I stopped to take a few pictures of the beautiful glaciers in the morning sun. As I started again, I was unable to catch up to Babu, Rob, and Mndeme, who had kept hiking. They were already a few yards ahead.

We reached Stella Point, halfway around the rim to the summit, and Babu was getting farther in front of me. My legs were getting heavier. My whole body ached with nausea. My mouth was unbearably dry and my throat scratched. I hadn't had anything to drink in hours. The tip of my water hose had frozen, and no matter how hard I tried, I could not get anything out of it.

Rob was taking a break in front of me with Ally, one of the assistant guides.

"Do you have any water you can spare?" I asked.

"Sure, no problem," Rob smiled. It was amazing to hear the difference between the lack of energy his body showed, and the life still in his voice. It was Rob's mental strength and enthusiasm that had carried him this far, and would continue to carry him the rest of the way. I knew he'd make it. He handed me a water bottle and I took a few sips. My stomach immediately protested, but I forced it down and it held. I gave the water to Ally and stumbled on. After another two hundred feet I was exhausted again and needed another break. Ally appeared again and I took the water bottle back and forced down the rest of the liter. *Water was all I needed*, I assured myself. *With a bit more hydration, I'll get my energy back and clear my head.*

Rob had walked on ahead, and Ally and I were alone now. Suddenly my head went light and my stomach exploded. I convulsed and immediately vomited the complete contents of my stomach. My whole body retched as the nausea I had fought for so long finally won, rejecting everything I had just put down. I spewed a full liter of water by the trail as Ally stood next to me, rubbing small circles on my back as I vomited everywhere. He never said a word. I heaved and retched several more times before my stomach was finally convinced it had expelled absolutely everything. Then I stood up, wiped my face, and began to walk.

My body was starting to crumble. I walked another hundred feet and needed to take a break. I walked again, and after another hundred feet, I needed to rest. As time dragged on, I got more and more tired. I began to fall asleep while standing up. It was almost impossible to keep my eyes open. I don't know where Ally went, but the next person I remembered seeing was Mndeme. He appeared out of nowhere, standing beside me.

"You are very tired." He looked at me. "You can't stay awake." He reached over to take my arm to help me and I stumbled backward as I held up my hand in protest.

"I can do it!" I tried to sound stronger than I felt. And I continued.

I don't know exactly when it happened or how it happened, but I finally found my mantra: *Leave it on the mountain.* These five words kept repeating like a tribal chant through my head. *Leave it on the mountain. Leave it on the mountain. Leave it on the mountain. Leave it on the mountain.*

The mantra rolled around in my head. I would leave every scrap of what I had on the mountain. I would take nothing with me. I would not save anything. If I had any amount of energy to give, I would give it to the mountain. *Chuck . . . chuck . . . step . . . step.* I would go for fifty or a hundred feet until my legs couldn't go any farther. Then I would sit down on a rock for a minute or two and get my energy back. Slowly I'd heft my body into standing and continue the cycle again.

Somewhere along the line, I met up with Paul, hunched over his trekking poles in front of me. He'd shuffle fifty feet and then stop and slump on his poles for a minute before starting up again. Given how little he'd eaten the past few days, I was amazed at how far he'd made it already. He was about twenty feet in front of me, and Mndeme stayed between us trying to help and keep an eye on both of us as we slowly advanced.

I looked up and saw a group of people on a rock formation. *That must be the summit*, I thought. I can definitely make it to there. *Chuck . . . chuck . . . step . . . step.* But just as we got to the rock formation, the trail veered to the right and along the inside of the crater rim.

It wasn't the summit. I stumbled in between the rocks and tried to maintain my balance. I looked up and saw Patricia, Carolyn, and Jim coming back from the summit. I stood up straight and mustered all the strength I could.

"You're almost there," Patricia said, encouraging me as she passed.

Once I got past the rocks, I could see another group of people sitting a few hundred feet down the trail. "Is that the summit?" I asked Mndeme weakly.

"Yes. You can see it from there."

My mind played with his reply for a moment. Did he mean that was the summit, or only that I could see the summit from there, or something else? I was too tired to question him further. I would find out once I got there. And, really, it didn't matter. If it wasn't the summit, I would just keep going until I got there.

Leave it on the mountain.
Leave it on the mountain.
Leave it on the mountain.

Well, it was not the summit. When I got to that point, I looked another half-mile down the trail and could see an even larger group standing and sitting around a tall sign. I could see the glaciers and the crater beyond that. That was the summit. I wasn't there yet.

Leave it on the mountain.
Chuck . . . chuck . . . step . . . step.
Leave it on the mountain.
Chuck . . . chuck . . . step . . . step.
Leave it on the mountain.
Chuck . . . chuck . . . step . . . step.

Every fifty feet or so, I would find a rock to sit on and recover. As soon as I sat down, my eyes would shut and I'd almost fall off the rock in a deep stupor before jolting myself back to consciousness. It was exhausting. Maybe Paul had a better system by resting on his poles, but I didn't have the capacity to question it.

Mndeme repeated his offer to help, but again I refused. I needed to do this on my own.

Leave it on the mountain.
Chuck . . . chuck . . . step . . . step.
Leave it on the mountain.
Chuck . . . chuck . . . step . . . step.
Leave it on the mountain.
Chuck . . . chuck . . . step . . . step.

Paul and I continued like this, neck and neck, with our guardian angel Mndeme following along to protect us, all the way to the summit. Finally, we made it.

Tim, Carmen, Rob, and Babu were all leaving the summit just as Paul and I arrived. "Congratulations," someone offered as they passed. "You made it," someone else said.

As Babu passed me on his way down, I leaned into him: "You're my inspiration."

"I'm glad I'm somebody's inspiration," he said and continued on.

When I got to the summit, I didn't yell, shout, cheer, or celebrate in any other way. I simply sat down and immediately fell asleep. But that didn't last long. That same part of my brain that had kept reciting my mantra immediately came up with a new one: *Don't fall asleep!*

I lurched upright in time to hear Mndeme tell me it was time to take my picture. I managed to stand up and walk to the sign just as another group of climbers cleared away. I squatted at the base to ensure Mndeme would get the whole thing in the picture. I dug deep and pulled up as much energy as I could to smile and make it look like I was actually enjoying myself. Mndeme snapped the picture. Thank God! I had made it.

Dr. Hans Meyer, the first climber ever to see the top of Kilimanjaro, was typically reserved. But he wrote effusively of the summit in *Across East African Glaciers*: "The ice fields flashed and glittered in the dazzling sunlight, the wind sighed whisperingly in the crannies and crevices, and in the depths of the yawning cauldron at our feet light wreaths of vapor curled softly and ceaselessly." Sounds pretty impressive, doesn't it?

I'm afraid I wouldn't know. When I reached the top, I was too exhausted and nauseous to enjoy the moment myself. Once Mndeme had taken the requisite summit photo, that was it. Meyer had celebrated with a couple of chocolate cakes and a cigarette. I celebrated by keeping my digestive tract from climbing up my throat.

Mndeme turned Paul and me around and started us back down the mountain. The glaciers were beautiful. The views spectacular. I yearned to take out my camera and snap a few photos, but I didn't have the energy and didn't want to keep Mndeme and Paul waiting. Already, we were moving painfully slow, the last ones on the mountain.

We had reached the summit and our goal, but we didn't gain any new strength with this achievement. Our progress was the same down as it had been going up.

Chuck . . . chuck . . . step . . . step.

Every fifty feet or so I slumped on a rock to rest, and Paul flopped over his trekking poles. As we stumbled down the path, I realized that I had lost my mantra. I had made it to the summit, then my mind started to wander. What was next? My thinking suddenly became very analytical. I evaluated my current situation in an almost out-of-body way.

I was completely exhausted. My body was breaking down with each step. I didn't have any energy left. No matter how strong the human will, eventually the body has a finite amount of energy. Once the body reached that point, it would simply stop functioning. It was that simple. I wasn't thinking about death quite so much as exhaustion. I hadn't had a drink of water I could keep down in more than four hours. I hadn't ingested a calorie in over eight hours. The math seemed pretty simple.

As I worked out this reality, I tried to explain it to Mndeme.

"You can sleep when we get to Gillman Point," he answered, and we kept going.

I knew that was the prudent thing. But I also knew I needed sleep. If I could just get a five-minute nap, I'd have the energy to make it to Gillman Point for my next nap. After that, I reasoned, I should have the energy to get all the way back down.

I decided to put this theory to a test. At my next rest point I sat on the ground and flopped onto my side on the cold dirt. As soon as I closed my eyes, though, a new wave of nausea filled my body. My stomach heaved as I could feel the whole earth spinning beneath me. My body and mind bickered

Glaciers on the summit of Kilimanjaro *(Photograph by Casey Lary)*

over which was worse—the lack of sleep or the horrible nausea. I opened my eyes to end the wretched feeling.

"Let's go. No sleep now," Mndeme said, pulling me to my feet. We continued. The trail dipped slightly and the minor descent was a wonderful respite. I was now able to make it a hundred feet at a time between stops. I felt stronger as our pace quickened with the decline. Unfortunately, the descent didn't last.

The final hundred feet to Gillman Point was uphill. The actual hill was probably only about fifty feet in elevation gain, but it seemed enormous. I knew I had to do it, and the fastest way to get over it was just to go. I tried to ride the downhill momentum into the uphill portion. But it didn't work. As soon as I took one step up the incline, my body revolted again. As I put my left leg forward and rocked my weight onto it, I felt like my thigh muscle ripped in two.

The pain was excruciating but also a new sensation. I had been cold, tired, exhausted, and nauseous. But this was the first time the entire day I had actually felt real pain and it was sobering. My mind rolled around the feeling, trying to decide if this was a real injury or just a new level of ache. My feet continued to trudge up the hill as my mind worked the problem. I wondered if this was a real threat to my ability to descend or just my body trying to get out of the last bit of work. Each time I stepped off my left leg, a shot went through my thigh. As I climbed the hill, my mind settled on the fact that it really didn't matter if my leg was actually hurt or not. I needed to get off this mountain. The only way to do that was to walk down it.

After a few more stops and some frantic grabs from Mndeme, I made it back to Gillman Point. Paul had gone on ahead a few feet and was waiting for us when we arrived. I slumped onto the ground, fondly remembering my deal with Mndeme to let me sleep. "Twenty minutes," I heard him say from the distance as I slid out of consciousness.

Before I knew it, it was time to get up. I lumbered onto my feet and hefted my trekking poles for the climb down. Paul had gone ahead and I could see him plodding along below us. The top portion of the descent was rocky, and the path wound between rocks and over boulders. It was hard going, but I was renewed from my nap. Each time I stepped too far down with my left leg, the pain strangled my thigh. But I didn't care. I found a new mantra: *Get to the bottom and you can sleep.*

It was all downhill from there. I found myself stopping less often and just pushing on through the pain and exhaustion. Every so often we'd hit an uneven part and I'd lose my balance. I'd take a short break and then continue. Finally we entered the sandy switchback portion. Then I really started to burn some miles. It was like walking down a snowy steep hill. With each large step down, my foot slid several feet in the sand before I'd plant my other foot and continue the momentum. I was almost skiing down the rocky grains, using my poles for balance. Most of my weight rested on my skeleton as I locked my knees and slid further. My muscles rejoiced in the reduced effort.

Paul was more than fifty feet ahead of me, but I was now closing the distance. With each step I skated farther down the steep decline, striking my poles and throwing my weight forward. I even started to get ahead of Mndeme as my new mode of transport invigorated me. The sun radiated down on us and the heat penetrated every layer of clothes I had piled on. Sweat streamed down my face and into my eyes. I stopped to tear off as many layers as possible. And then I plodded forward.

By the time I got to the bottom, I had finally caught up with Paul. It was suddenly very important to me to keep pace. Paul had trained by running three marathons and here we were, coming off the mountain together. I let myself hope that maybe, if I was able to keep up with someone this physically and mentally tough, then maybe it was okay that I came down last in our group.

We hit the trailhead with only a half-mile to go and we were baking. My legs were pooling sweat into my boots. I shuffled along the last bit as fast as my weary legs would carry me with Mndeme and Paul right behind. "Do you know the name of that rock formation?" I heard Paul ask Mndeme. I was dumbfounded. I knew Paul was half dead from his Herculean effort on the mountain. And now, at the end of it all, he had the wherewithal to ask about the rocks? All I could think about was sleep and he was interested in the scenery. I couldn't help but admire his endurance and enthusiasm.

The three of us entered Kibo Camp just before noon. We had been hiking nonstop for twelve hours. The rest of the group was already there and all gave a cheer at our arrival. Mike and Tim snapped a quick picture of our triumphant return before Patricia took Paul away.

I was completely exhausted and thoroughly pleased with myself. I had earned a nice long rest. I climbed into my tent and tore off my sweaty thermals. I shoved away my sleeping bag and flopped onto my air mattress. It was heaven. I could finally sleep.

"Um . . . Daniel?" I heard from behind. I looked up and saw Mndeme and Mohamed peeking into my tent. "Sorry, you can only sleep for one hour. After that we must leave."

"Fine," I replied, and then I immediately fell into a deep sleep.

At one point Mike looked in and roused me with some hot soup and juice. "You should eat something." He reached into the tent with a steaming bowl.

"No thanks," I mumbled and fell back to sleep.

Mike roused me again after an hour and a half. "They need to pack up everything," he said. "This is the last tent. We really need to start moving."

I rolled over. I didn't want to get up. I didn't want to eat. I just wanted to sleep for a long time. But Mike was right: we needed to move if we'd have any hope of getting to the lower Horombu Camp before dark. I flopped onto my side and pulled over my water bottle. I slurped down the remaining sports drink and waited to see if it would stay down. After a few moments I was mildly confident it wasn't going to spring back up my throat. My body immediately absorbed the hydration and the calories and I felt a little bit better. I sipped some more water and nibbled on some of the food Mike had left out for me.

I began to pack up my things and prepare to move out. I found every minor task monumental. It took me over an hour to stuff some clothes into my backpack and an eternity to get my sleeping bag into the tiny stuffsack. Normally this took twenty minutes. I stumbled out of the tent and saw Babu and Mike patiently waiting for me on a nearby rock. They were completely packed and ready to go. Mine was the only tent still standing. Everyone else had already moved on.

I hefted my daypack onto my weary shoulders and we set off with Mndeme for the final stretch of the day. I knew it wasn't going to be easy. We had ten miles to go before we could rest again. It was all downhill, but it seemed like a hell of a long way to walk on my still wobbly legs.

We hiked out of Kibo Camp and descended into the saddle between Kibo and Mawenzi. The landscape had a barren and silent beauty to match the craggy spires of Mawenzi to our left. The trail was basically a dirt road, smooth and flat. It descended at a nice, slow, gradual pace that made the hike bearable, actually enjoyable.

We were alone now. There were no other climbers hiking down from Kibo this late, and all the climbers ascending had already passed. It felt like we had the whole mountain to ourselves. The wind gently pushed at our backs as the road rose up beneath us. Yes, it pretty much felt like an Irish blessing at that point. It was also nice to have some alone time with Mike and his father. For the most part we had been stuck in a large mob for the past six days. This was the first time we had the trail to ourselves. No one else was anywhere in sight.

"So, Babu, how do you feel about your climb?" I asked.

"I feel pretty good about it," he replied with some modesty.

"Do you feel proud of what you've accomplished?"

"No, not pride. I'm just happy with what I've achieved."

"What about you, Mike?" I asked.

Mike looked around the lovely East African scene and soaked it all in for a moment. He looked back at the summit and the miles we had already covered since leaving camp. "You know, it really doesn't get much better than this. I had a great time. I got to spend time with my best friend and my father. I met some interesting people. And I climbed higher than I've ever been in my entire life. Not bad."

No, it wasn't bad at all. In fact, we felt euphoric. Of course, that could have been the increased oxygen going to our brains as we descended to the lower elevations. I was still exhausted but also feeling better with each step down. After a few miles we transitioned into the alpine meadow landscape and saw the return of green grasses, sage, and small wildflowers. It was even more beautiful for having been absent for the past three days. We crossed a small stream where stubby giant groundsel trees sprang from the surrounding meadow. The trail turned from a dirt road to rocky tracks. The uneven ground and protruding stones made hiking harder and required more focus to keep from falling on my face.

As we made our way into the heather brush, Mndeme tried to teach us a few new words in Swahili.

"How do you say 'I'm beat'?" I asked.

"What do you mean 'beat'?" he inquired.

"It means really, really tired, completely exhausted. No energy at all."

"Ahh," he replied. "*Choka sana.*"

"*Choka sana?*"

"Yes, you would say, '*Nime choka sana.*'"

Mndeme spelled it for me and I wrote it in my notebook to ensure I wouldn't forget it. The guides and porters had patiently taught us several Swahili words over the course of our time together, but at this point I couldn't remember any of them.

We entered Horombu Camp by 6:00 PM. We had spent the past eighteen hours hiking from 15,340 feet above sea level up to 19,340 feet and then all the way down to 12,200 feet, roughly eighteen miles in all. The air felt thick with oxygen and my tired body drank it all in. Horombu Camp is the second camp along the Marangu Route and climbers ascending and descending both stay here. Unlike the other routes this one actually has huts. Climbers can ascend the mountain and spend their nights sleeping in real wooden structures on real wooden beds with real mattresses. The huts look more like ski lodges; shaped in a tall brown triangle to shed the snow. Many of the huts actually have curtains in the front windows, like deluxe vacation rentals in the Alps.

Since we had not ascended via the Marangu Route, we couldn't use the huts. We propped our tents on the same small plot of land. I could see why Marangu was commonly referred to as the Coca-Cola Route. The rest of our group was already sitting in the dining tent drinking their first beers. This was way too civilized. The porters were fast at work preparing dinner and boiling water for hot tea. We reached our tents and immediately Juma came over.

"Water for washing," he said with a grin.

"*Nime choka sana,*" I replied and was immediately rewarded with a howl of laughter.

"*Nime choka sana,*" Juma said back to me in complete agreement.

I made it!

11

Leave It on the Mountain

The suffering was finally over. We were done for the day, and I didn't need to take another step if I didn't want to. That was good, because every time I lifted my left leg, my thigh muscles screamed in absolute agony, perhaps in punishment for subjecting them to this mountain again. Mike and I settled into our tent before he went off to see how the others were doing, and I lay down for a short nap before dinner. I could have happily curled up until morning, but I had one more day of hiking. I needed those calories.

Mohamed poked into my tent. "Dinner," he commanded. I slogged over to the dining tent, joining the others. Everyone was tired but generally feeling good. Rob and Tim appeared to be getting quickly drunk on a bottle of warm beer they had procured from someone.

"Hell, that's the best part," Rob said. "When you're at 12,000 feet it only takes one beer to get you drunk. Thank God the Diamox didn't make me not like beer." He toasted his good fortune and downed a gulp. Rob had good reason to celebrate. He had been offered the option to turn back, but instead he'd charged on and made it to the top.

"Mohamed wouldn't let me quit," Rob admitted. "I was getting ready to go down but Mohamed just wouldn't let me. When Mohamed tells you to do something, you don't argue. Especially at 19,000 feet."

Soon Paul, Carolyn, and Jim filed in for dinner. They were all exhausted and had hoped to skip food for sleep. "Mohamed told us we had to come to dinner," Paul mumbled.

Juma served up some onion soup followed by rice and beans. The bland starches were a welcome addition to my empty but still queasy stomach. Dinner was sedate, with muted conversations that went silent as we forced down our meal. We drifted off to bed as soon as we were finished, and the moment my head hit the wad of clothing I called a pillow I was out. It was the deepest sleep I think I've ever had—I was completely comatose until late the next morning.

The sun was already well above the horizon by the time I emerged from my tent. My muscles were still fatigued, but it was the ache of success, and I didn't mind. I packed up the last of my smelly clothes and strapped on my clunky hiking boots for the final hike. The porters snatched up all the bags and shot out of camp with loads balanced on their heads. We marched out behind them in a long, straggling line.

The hike out was surprisingly beautiful. Shortly after leaving Horombu Camp, we entered the rain forest and spent our last few hours on Kilimanjaro surrounded by sweeping vines, bursting wildflowers, and lush foliage. Small brooks of crystal water and tiny waterfalls nestled along the path as we descended. We heard the sounds of birds and monkeys overhead while small critters rustled in the brush just out of sight beside us. I slowed down to enjoy the forest, hiking at the back of the group with Tim and Mndeme. It was nice to be able to enjoy the mountain and the company of my fellow travelers again now that the pressure of the summit was finally behind me.

By late afternoon we arrived at the Marangu Gate and the climb was officially over. We bought cold sodas and sat on the steps of the small park service office. Mohamed handed out summit certificates to everyone—everyone except for Mike.

"Did Mike make it to Gillman Point?" Mohamed asked me. I was pretty certain Mohamed knew how far Mike had gone, but he was giving us a second chance. I pondered for a moment. Mike had gone far and accomplished a lot. Certainly his effort deserved some kind of recognition.

I turned to Mike. "Mohamed is filling out the certificates. Did you make it to Gillman Point?" I clarified. "Do you want a certificate for Gillman Point?"

"No thanks," Mike replied, sitting tall. "I don't need a certificate."

After a final group photo we boarded the bus that would take us back to Moshi. We pulled through the black metal gate into the hotel compound and the wheels crunched across the gravel driveway announcing our return. Lisa ran out to greet us. As soon as she saw me, she smiled. She knew that I had made it.

"Congratulations!" she called out. I wrapped my weary arms around her and held her tight. It seemed as though I hadn't seen her in years. I looked upon her with different eyes, eyes from three years ago, when we had first dreamed about Africa together. We were together again, in that beautiful place without the pressure of the mountain hanging between us.

"You think you want to climb Everest next?" she asked with a wry smile.

"Nope. This was my Everest." I was done. The mountain was behind us and we could now just enjoy East Africa. Lisa and I spent the next week with the group, exploring the exotic countryside on safari. During the day we rode through game parks, taking photos of the magnificent wildlife. In the evenings we sipped beers by the fire, basking in the glory of our accomplishments, and talking about other adventures past and future.

As soon as we returned to Moshi, everyone hurried to the airport and back to civilization. Lisa and I stayed on a bit longer. We were on Tanzanian time now. We chatted with other climbers, wandered along the streets of Moshi, and picked up a few extra gifts to take home. We weren't ready to say good-bye.

The next night we sat quietly at Kilimanjaro Airport waiting for our flight. It seemed strange to be leaving. All that had happened since my first date with Lisa at Diedrich's Coffee Shop now seemed like a dream. Since then, we'd been to Africa twice, been married, and moved across the world. I had climbed the highest peak on the African continent, the first of the Seven Summits. If not for the pictures, I'm not sure I would have believed it.

Tanzania now felt like a second home to us. The people were so warm and welcoming that on this second trip, it felt more like we were visiting family than taking a vacation. I was forever connected to this place and I was sad to leave it. From Tanzania I had learned the lesson of laughter and the value of finding happiness even in the face of adversity. From Kilimanjaro I had learned to dig deep and find strength I never knew I had, to live life fully.

I had been to the top of Kilimanjaro, but I hadn't conquered it. It had conquered me. The mountain had taught me my personal mantra. The phrase had stuck with me even a week after the summit. *Leave it on the mountain.* It was a powerful life lesson that I'd carry with me for years to come. I would live my life fully, giving everything I have. I wouldn't hold back anything. If I chose to climb a mountain again, figuratively or literally, I would embrace the challenge fully and give everything I have to it. My coworker Delphine had been right after all: Kilimanjaro was a life-changing experience.

As we took off, I watched as the monitor displayed our progress skyward into the night. It took the plane just under five minutes to pass 19,000 feet. It had taken me more than three years.

Two days later, Lisa and I sat down for dinner back in Germany, a world away from Tanzania. The phone rang. It was my younger brother calling from the States. "Congratulations! So you finally made it. Good for you."

"Thanks, Matt," I replied. At last, I was ready to face the world. I had actually stood on the summit of Mount Kilimanjaro. From now on, when anyone asked about my climbing attempt, all I had to say was: "I made it." That would be that. No more questions, no more explanations, no more justifications. I had made it to the top, and that accomplishment excluded me from any further explanations. I was done, thank God.

Or so I thought. "But hey," my brother asked, "if it's so hard, how come Mike's seventy-three-year-old father made it on his first try?"

Recommended Reading

Bryson, Bill. *Bill Bryson's African Diary*. New York: Broadway Books. 2002.

Burns, Cameron M. *Kilimanjaro and East Africa: A Climbing and Trekking Guide*, 2nd edition. Seattle: The Mountaineers Books. 2006

Burton, Richard F. *First Footsteps in East Africa: or, An Exploration of Harar*. Mineola, NY: Dover Publications. 1987.

Hartley, Aidan. *The Zanzibar Chest: A Story of Life, Love, and Death in Foreign Lands*. New York: Riverhead Trade. 2004.

Martin, David. *Manyara: Tanzania National Parks*. Arusha, Tanzania: Tanzania National Parks. 2001.

_____. *Serengeti: Tanzania*. Arusha, Tanzania: Tanzania National Parks. 1997.

Meyer, Hans. *Across East African Glaciers: An Account of the First Ascent of Kilimanjaro*. Trans. E.H.S. Calder. Whitefish, MT: Kessinger Publications. 2007.

Reader, John. *Africa: A Biography of the Continent*. New York: Vintage. 1999.

Ridgeway, Rick. *The Shadows of Kilimanjaro: On Foot Across East Africa*. New York: Holt Paperbacks. 1999.

Saitoti, Tepilit Ole. *The Worlds of a Maasai Warrior*. Trans: John Galaty. Berkeley: University of California Press. 1988.

Salkeld, Audrey. *Kilimanjaro: To The Roof of Africa*. Washington, DC: National Geographic. 2002.

Stedman, Henry. *Kilimanjaro: The Trekking Guide to Africa's Highest Mountain*, 2nd edition. Surrey, England: Trailblazer. 2006.

Theroux, Paul. *Dark Star Safari: Overland from Cairo to Cape Town*. New York: Mariner Books. 2004.

Zeleza, Tiyambe. *Maasai*. New York: Rosen Publishing Group. 1994.

About the Author

Daniel Dorr thinks of himself as no one in particular; an ordinary guy who has been fortunate enough to have some very extraordinary experiences. After undergraduate school he lived in Japan for a year teaching English and American culture to Japanese high-school students while trying to learn Aikido and Kendo after school. After his return to the States he became a "salary man," living and working in New Orleans, New York City, San Jose, California, Lake Tahoe Nevada, and eventually Germany.

Along the way he still managed to have a few adventures: rock climbing in Yosemite National Park, the Alps and the Philippines; working on a dairy farm in western New York; and traveling to East Africa for a climb or two.

After his family, his next great love is exploring. Now that he has two young daughters he just needs to remember to bring the diaper bag with him when he hits the trail.

Connect with Daniel and other Kilimanjaro adventurers at www.kiliadventures.com.

THE MOUNTAINEERS, founded in 1906, is a nonprofit outdoor activity and conservation club, whose mission is "to explore, study, preserve, and enjoy the natural beauty of the outdoors. . . ." Based in Seattle, Washington, the club is now one of the largest such organizations in the United States, with seven branches throughout Washington State.

The Mountaineers sponsors both classes and year-round outdoor activities in the Pacific Northwest, which include hiking, mountain climbing, ski-touring, snowshoeing, bicycling, camping, canoeing and kayaking, nature study, sailing, and adventure travel. The club's conservation division supports environmental causes through educational activities, sponsoring legislation, and presenting informational programs.

All club activities are led by skilled, experienced volunteers, who are dedicated to promoting safe and responsible enjoyment and preservation of the outdoors.

If you would like to participate in these organized outdoor activities or the club's programs, consider a membership in The Mountaineers. For information and an application, write or call The Mountaineers, Club Headquarters, 7700 Sand Point Way NE, Seattle, WA 98115; 206-521-6001. You can also visit the club's website at www.mountaineers.org or contact The Mountaineers via email at clubmail@mountaineers.org.

The Mountaineers Books, an active, nonprofit publishing program of the club, produces guidebooks, instructional texts, historical works, natural history guides, and works on environmental conservation. All books produced by The Mountaineers Books fulfill the club's mission. Visit www.mountaineersbooks.org to find details about all our titles and the latest author events, as well as videos, web clips, links, and more!

 The Mountaineers Books
1001 SW Klickitat Way, Suite 201
Seattle, WA 98134
800-553-4453
mbooks@mountaineersbooks.org

916.7826/00R
CITY LIBRARY

**OTHER TITLES YOU MIGHT ENJOY FROM
THE MOUNTAINEERS BOOKS**

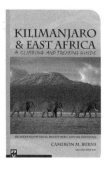

**Kilimanjaro and East Africa: A Climbing
and Trekking Guide, 2nd Edition**
By Cameron M. Burns
Climb East Africa's highest peaks—via non-technical
and technical routes—with this updated guide to
Kilimanjaro, Mount Kenya, and more.

**Walking The Gobi: A 1600-Mile Trek
Across a Desert of Hope and Despair**
By Helen Thayer
Baby-boomer and adventurer Helen Thayer
tells the remarkable story of her 1600-mile trek
across the Gobi Desert. Fierce temperatures, drug
smugglers, inhospitable terrain, and natural
history mark her journey.

**High Infatuation: A Climber's Guide
to Love and Gravity**
By Steph Davis
One of the most accomplished female rock
climbers in the world takes readers along
as she climbs, struggles, loves, and makes
it to the top.

Forget Me Not: A Memoir
Jennifer Lowe-Anker; foreword by Jon Krakauer
An insightful and at times wrenching memoir of
love lost and love found, set against a backdrop
of the world's tallest peaks.

**The Tecate Journals: Seventy Days
on the Rio Grande**
By Keith Bowden
More than a man-against-nature adventure,
The Tecate Journals reveals the complex reality of
the Rio Grande.

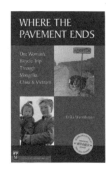

**Where The Pavement Ends: One Woman's
Bicycle Trip Through Mongolia, China &
Vietnam**
By Erika Warmbrunn
One woman's amazing 8000-kilometer cycling
adventure through the
splendor of Asia.

**The Mountaineers Books has more than
500 outdoor recreation titles in print.**
For details, visit
www.mountaineersbooks.org.